Dialogue & Initiative
2015 Edition

Racism, Austerity, and the Struggle for 21st Century Socialism

Published by the
Committees of Correspondence Education Fund

Changemaker Publications

Dialogue & Initiative is a discussion journal published by the Committees of Correspondence Education Find, Inc.,

2526 Broadway New York, NY 10025-5654

646-942-7951

Email: national@cc-ds.org
Web: www.cc-ds.org

Co-Editors: Erica Carter, Paul Krehbiel, Harry Targ

Editorial Committee: Carl Davidson, Pat Fry, Ted Reich, Janet Tucker

Layout and design for this issue: Carl Davidson,

Manuscripts not exceeding 5000 words are invited. Send text via email; hard copy can be mailed or faxed. Manuscripts will be returned if acompanied by postage-paid, self-addressed packaging.

Copyright: CoC Ed Fund, May 2015, unless otherwise reserved by the authors.

ISBN# 978-1-329-15774-3
Order online direct at:
http://www.lulu.com/spotlight/changemaker

Table on Contents

Part One: Structural Racism

Racism, the Criminal Justice System, and Civilian Police Accountability, by Harry Targ, Page 1

What Is Our Attitude Toward the Present Youth-Led Rebellion? by Frank Chapman, Page 4

Racism, Police Murders, and Mass Incarceration Have Roots In Capitalism, by Alex Krehbiel, Page 7

Rage Against the Narrative: How To Understand Psychic Violence & Murder. by Lisa Brock, Page 14

Police Violence, Capital & Neoliberalism, by Gary Potter, Page 19

Color Blindness in the Age of Escalating Racism, by Ted Pearson, page 27

Digna And Me: Cuba, Race And Transnational Solidarity, by Lisa Brock, Page 30

The Coercive State in Contemporary Capitalism, by Jim Grant, Daniel Mejia and Zach Robinson, Page 36

Part Two: Austerity

The Fusion Politics Response to 21st Century Imperialism: From Arab Spring to Moral Mondays, by Harry Targ, Page 49

New Developments In Labor: The Fight Against Racism, Injustice & Austerity, by Paul Krehbiel, Page 75

Growers to Gut California's Farm Labor Law, by David Bacon, Page 86

How Many Governments Can Boast 83% Approval Rating by Their People? The Greek People Rise Up, By Aris Anagnos, Page 97

A Sympathetic Critique of Naomi Klein's '*This Changes Everything*', by David Schwartzman, Page 100

Lies and Myths About Greece and Europe's Debt, by Conn Hallinan, Page 103

PDA, the Congressional Progressive Caucus and the People's Budget, by Randy Shannon, Page 108

American Sniper, Why So Popular?, by Lila Garrett, Page 113

Is the United States Inching Towards Fascism?, by Mark Solomon, Page 116

Part Three: The Struggle for 21st Century Socialism

Eleven Talking Points on 21st Century Socialism, by Carl Davidson, Page 122

Getting Past Capitalism, by Cynthia Kaufman Page 127

Book Review: '*A World To Build: New Paths Towards 21st Century Socialism,*' by Marta Harnecker, Monthly Review Press, 2015, by Duncan McFarland, Page 131

Draft of an 8-Point Platform for Making a Major Breakthrough on 'Left Unity', by Carl Davidson, Bill Fletcher, Jr. and Pat Fry, Page 135

Cooperative Cuba, by Cliff DuRand, Page 138

LeftRoots: Towards A Transformational Strategy, By N'Tanya

Lee, Cinthya Muñoz, Maria Poblet, Josh Warren-White and Steve Williams, Page 146

CCDS Statement on Solidarity with Vietnam, Page 155

40th Anniversary of End of War in Vietnam: A Photo Essay By Ted Reich, Page 157.

Introduction: Racism, Austerity & the Struggle for 21st Century Socialism

As we put these words to the page and you, the reader, peruse them, other African Americans are being shot, tortured, and/or humiliated by policemen who have gotten away with these crimes with impunity. The string of murders is long and getting longer, with hundreds of Blacks killed by white cops every year. One recent killing turned out a little different. On April 4, 2015, Walter Scott, an unarmed Black man, was shot repeatedly in the back by a white cop, Michael Slager, in North Charleston, South Carolina. The police department found no wrong doing, until a video tape of the murder appeared, filmed by a bystander. Only then, was Slager charged with murder.

But in all the scores of murders of Black men by white police before the murder of Walter Scott, no charges have been filed against the murderers. The cops continue their killing spree, apparently feeling that they can murder at will and nothing will be done to them. On April 12, 2015, Freddie Gray, an unarmed Black man, was arrested by Baltimore police, manhandled and thrown into a police van. Gray's pleas for medical attention were ignored. He died in police custody on April 19 of a severe spinal injury. On April 24, 2015, during the funeral for Freddie Gray, frustration and anger boiled over in the streets of Baltimore. Rioting broke out. Both police and demonstrators were hurt, and protestors arrested. The Baltimore Orioles baseball game had to be cancelled. The Crips and Bloods street gangs of Baltimore, usually mortal enemies, announced a truce to unite to protest police killings of Blacks.

The open, public murder of African Americans by white police officers is an outrage. Blacks are 21 times more likely to be killed by police than whites, according to ProPublica, even though African Americans make up just 13% of the US population. The mass protests against these killings were sparked by the brutal slaying of Michael Brown in Ferguson in the summer, 2014. Mass protests against police murder have spread across the country.

These police murders underscore the structural racism that affects every aspect of life in the United States. As Angela Davis and others have pointed out, racism has been deeply embedded in the very fiber of US institutions since the first slaves disembarked from ships bringing human chattel to the "new world." The first stage of capitalism, primitive accumulation, was based on the kidnapping of men and women from Africa and transporting them as cattle to the "new world," after conquering the land and indigenous people living on it. This, as Marx related sarcastically, "was the happy dawn of civilization," a capitalist "civilization" that enriched the elite at the expense of the vast majority. While African Americans have borne the brunt of this brutally racist capitalist system, Latinos and other people of color, and people of many nationalities have been targeted as well. The goal by the capitalist elite rulers is to divide the working class in order to weaken it. Our goal is to unite it.

We focus in this issue of Dialogue & Initiative on discrimination, murder and incarceration of Black men. We must also remember that equally important are the assaults on Black women, Latinos, Asians, Muslims and all who suffer discrimination, beatings, jailing, and murder. The historical trajectory is clear. The murder of Michael Brown is inextricably linked to the kidnappings, the slave system, the lynchings, and "the new Jim Crow" of massive incarceration linking the past to the present. And each new development of racism was necessitated and reinforced by the full flowering of the capitalist system such that race and class have been connected as one in the United States. Both institutionalized racism and capitalism, in the end, have to be eliminated to allow for the full flowering of human wellbeing.

Centrality of Racism

This issue of Dialogue and Initiative begins with several articles that address the issue of institutionalized racism and how it can and must be challenged. Essays show the connections between capitalism, neoliberalism, and police malfeasance. They show how racism affects the electoral system, human psychology, police conduct, the criminalization and imprisonment of especially Black youth, and the many campaigns to stop the murder and abuse.

We continue with articles that address the struggles against austerity. They begin with the assumption that imposing austerity to the extent possible is intrinsic to capitalism and through the imposition of neoliberal policies, including downsizing governments and privatizing public institutions, resistance movements arise. The results have been devastating. The top global 1% will own more wealth than the other 99% of the world's people by 2016 if current trends continue, according to a recent report by Oxfam, an international organization working to combat poverty, hunger, and injustice. The articles in Dialogue & Initiative describe how social movements, including the renewal of the labor movement, anti-racism campaigns, the fight to save the environment, for immigrant rights, and electoral contests have emerged over the last three years in the United States and all across the globe.

The struggles against racism and austerity have been generating alternative visions of how to transform the present to a better future, to 21st century socialism. In the final section, articles address ways to envision socialism, challenge capitalism from within it, include the emergence of cooperatives as an alternative form of workplace democracy, and explore important debates about how the traditional and newer left forces can come together to build twenty first century socialism. Recent polls by the Pew organization show that one-third of our people are open to socialism. That number goes up to half for our youth, and half among members of the Democratic Party. Equally significant numbers of people of color and the working-class have a similar openness to socialism. We are in a new period, where we can and must talk about socialism. The deep and serious problems of capitalism are recurring because they are inherent in the capitalist system. Improvements can be made through the force of political movements. But these deep problems and serious crimes can only finally be resolved under socialism.

We hope that the analyses about structural racism, austerity, and the struggle for 21st century socialism can be used to educate, agitate, organize, and facilitate a deepening discussion and growing unity of political action around these key issues.

We end with a statement of solidarity with Vietnam on the 40th Anniversary of its total liberation from US imperialist war and occupation, and a short photo essay to remind us of the powerful anti-war movement that was developed in the United States to assist the Vietnamese in winning their freedom and independence. May the Vietnamese struggle for independence and the example of anti-war solidarity provide an example that victory is possible.

The Editors

Erica Carter, Co-Editor

Paul Krehbiel, Co-Editor

Harry Targ, Co-Editor

Part One: Structural Racism

Racism, the Criminal Justice System, and Civilian Police Accountability

By Harry Targ

Over the last several years the criminal justice systems at the federal, state, and local levels have threatened the basic rights of citizens, particularly people of color and youth. These violations of equal treatment under the law have included:

• A "national epidemic" of police and vigilante killings of young African American men. For example, Trayvon Martin and Jordan Davis in Florida, Eric Garner in New York City, Oscar Grant in Oakland, California, Michael Brown in Ferguson, Missouri, John Crawford III in Dayton, Ohio, Vonderrit Myers, Jr. in St. Louis, and Ezell Ford in Los Angeles.

• The mass incarceration of people of color such that, as Michelle Alexander has reported in her recent book, The New Jim Crow, more African Americans are in jail or under the supervision of the criminal justice system today than were in slavery in 1850;

• The institutionalization of laws increasing surveillance;

• The passage of so-called Stand Your Ground laws, justifying gun violence against people perceived as a threat.

On August 9, 2014 unarmed nineteen-year-old African American Michael Brown was shot multiple times by a Ferguson, Missouri policeman. In response to the collective expression of community outrage that followed, the local police initiated a multi-day barrage of tear gas, strong-arm arrests, and the threatening of street protestors with military vehicles and loaded rifles. The images on television screens nationwide were of a people under assault. The fear that young African American males in Ferguson have historically felt every time they stepped into the streets of their city was heightened by the killing of Michael Brown.

Significant events since that police murder have been protests, the visit to the Ferguson community by Attorney General Eric Holder and national mobilizations in Ferguson and around the country. Subsequent to that police killing, many more African American men have been killed by police officers across the nation. However, recent "testimony" leaked from the grand jury investigating the police crime has appeared in the St Louis Post-Dispatch and Washington Post that promotes a narrative that the police officer who murdered Brown was acting in self-defense.

Abuse Occurs Regularly

Along with police killings, other police abuse occurs regularly. In Hammond, Indiana, on September 24, 2014, an African American woman, who was the driver of a car and mother of two children in the back seat, and an adult male friend in the front passenger seat, was pulled over by a police officer for a seat belt violation. Fortunately nobody died, but the policeman drew his weapon and shattered the automobile's front side window. The policeman had ordered the male to roll down the window, tasered and then arrested him while the seven year old daughter of the driver cried in the back seat. Subsequently, Hammond authorities have defended the conduct of the police officer.

In a recently released study, journalists discovered that between 2010 and 2012 young Black males were shot to death by police 21 times more often than young whites. Their data was limited to those two years because earlier information accumulated by the FBI was incomplete. Prior to that time police departments had not filed required reports when police used force.

Even though data is partial, Professor Colin Loftin, co-director of the Violence Research Group, University of Alabama, said, "No question, there are all kinds of racial disparities across our criminal justice system." (Ryan Gabrielson, Ryann Grochowski Jones, and Eric Sagara, "Deadly Force, in Black and White," http://www.propublica.org/article/deadly-force-in-Black-and-white, October 10, 2014).

A growing body of evidence suggests that the criminal justice system administers justice in an unfair way - from general police/community relations, to trials and incarceration, to the use of violence and deadly force against minority youth.

While police are supposed to serve the interests of the communities in which they work, compelling evidence suggests that, to the contrary, force is used to stifle dissent and challenge assertions of political and cultural autonomy. The data overwhelmingly supports the conclusion that police systems are institutionalized forms of racism.

In response to racist police violence the Chicago Alliance Against Racist and Political Repression (CAARPR), a branch of the National Alliance, founded in 1973, has been working to "stop police crimes," establish "prison reform," and to oppose the incarceration of persons wrongfully incarcerated including political prisoners.

The CAARPR has proposed the establishment of a Civilian Police Accountability Council (CPAC) for the city. According to the plan, the city would create an elected CPAC which would oversee the personnel and policy of the police department. CPAC would appoint the Superintendent of Police, revise rules for police practices, investigate police misconduct, investigate all police shootings, and provide for transparency in investigations. The central premise of the CPAC idea is that the police exist to serve the community, not oppose it.

Real community control of police and the criminal justice system is basic to any democracy. Along with the generalized declining perception by Americans about the legitimacy of political institutions, minorities and youth see the police more as an occupying army than a force for protecting the safety, security, and independence of members of their community.

Harry Targ is a professor of Political Science at Purdue University, and a member of the National Executive Committee of the Committees of Correspondence for Democracy and Socialism.

What Is Our Attitude Toward the Present Youth-Led Rebellion?

By Frank Chapman

Due to the impetus of the present youth-led rebellion, our movement for community control of the police is moving from being a marginal community-based movement among African Americans to a broad democratic demand of the masses led by our Black youth nationally and internationally.

The National Alliance Against Racism and Political Repression's participation in this mass struggle is subordinated to the fundamental task of organizing a mass campaign for an all-civilian, elected Civilian Police Accountability Council (CPAC). Our attitude is that we are truly grateful for the mass youth-led uprisings that have given us these opportunities to fulfil our historic task of getting CPAC enacted by the Chicago City Council.

In this new year of struggle against police crimes and struggle for community control of the police we want to raise this question: What is the significance of the present uprising and what is our attitude toward it?

Our attitude was succinctly expressed by our comrade Larry Redmond at a recent community symposium. Regarding the present youth-led uprising Larry said: "This is what we have been waiting for and fighting for."

For the last two years we have been actively engaged in organizing mass protest against police crimes and calling upon the people to rise up; but this present movement was not a response to our calls. It was and is a spontaneous uprising of the masses that quickly, in hot house fashion, grew into organized mass protest. This is a democratic uprising whose minimal demand is that police who commit crimes should be charged, tried and punished for the crimes they commit; and whose maximum demand is the creation of an all-elected, all-civilian police accountability council or control board.

The youth who are leading this uprising realize that in confronting the police and the entire criminal justice system, they must position themselves to overturn racist institutions that are historically rooted in the long and cruel oppression of African Americans. In this endeavor they have called everybody out, thus ushering in the broadest, deepest democratic, anti-racist struggle that we have seen in decades. They have demonstrated their ability to move large masses of the population against police violence and tyranny, and to stop the flow of business as usual.

There have been mass social upheavals in the past fueled by the democratic aspirations of the masses but several decades have gone by since we have seen such a mass response to police-directed racist violence against African Americans. The struggle against police brutality is not new but this particular stage and phase of the struggle is new.

Here is how Mychal Denzel Smith, a writer for *The Nation* magazine, characterizes the present youth rebellion: "This new movement is being led by mostly young Black women who won't allow us to forget that Black women's lives matter. It is drawing in diverse crowds, including white allies who are not calling for gradual change, but a total end to white supremacy. The movement doesn't look or sound like anything our elders remember (or were taught) about the civil rights era. And that's OK. We have a new fight. We have to create a new model of resistance."

What is new about the present struggle is not the call for "a total end to white supremacy". In fact the "Black Power" movement of the 1960s did call for a total end of white supremacy. No one young or old in our movement would argue that the struggle to overturn white supremacy is new. Nor is the heroic struggle of Black youth from the high school students of Birmingham to the students murdered at Jackson State University new in our movement. Young people of yesterday (and many were killed from the 16 Street Baptist Church in Birmingham to Fred Hampton in Chicago) paved the way for the youth of today.

Must Concretely Identify What is New

If we really want to understand where we are in the present stage of our struggle, then we must concretely identify what is new and unprecedented based on accurate historical information. What is new about the present uprising is not the vital need of immediate elementary human rights embodied in the slogan Black Lives Matter but the rapidity with which this cry for justice has taken hold and united all the various strands of the peoples' movement and every section of the population. This movement generated, almost overnight, a mass united democratic front against racist police killings and their cover up by prosecutors. Through mass united actions in the streets here and around the world, people are demanding justice for Michael Brown and Eric Garner. This is unprecedented and that, in essence, is what is characteristically new about this movement in its present phase. So the burning question of our CPAC campaign is what actions we will take to consciously help this movement in its transition to political struggle.

There is an old saying that fashion drags hopelessly at the tail of life and so mass protest without specific political demands for policy changes aimed at bringing about systemic change drags hopelessly at the tail of piecemeal reforms and spends itself out; then repression returns with a vengeance.

There are at least two actions we believe we must take at once: 1) We must continue united action with the various contingents of this youth-led movement and respect their leadership. 2) We must continue and intensify community organizing through protests, demonstrations, forums, mass rallies, teach-ins, door-to-door canvassing, etc., for an all-elected, all-civilian police accountability council.

Need for Concrete Demands

In a society based on race and class oppression the struggle between oppressors and oppressed must ultimately become a struggle with concrete political demands. What kind of concrete demands should we form our fight around? The kind that leads to systemic change; fighting for the enactment of laws where the oppressed are empowered; fighting for the forming of a council where people elect members of their communities to a form of direct local government that has the power to hold police accountable and puts the process of deciding/controlling policing policies into the hands of oppressed communities. Such a path, where we fight for community control of the police is also an important step in the direction of turning the political arena into an arena of mass-based democratic struggles for further systemic changes.

We are presently engaged in planning and developing our part in this struggle. We encourage you to join us.

Frank Chapman is Field Secretary of the Chicago Alliance Against Racist and Political Repression

Racism, Police Murders, and Mass Incarceration Have Roots In Capitalism

By Alex Krehbiel

The ongoing protests against police murders of Black people and other people of color that have been taking place across the country is a progressive and hopeful phenomenon.

This multi-racial movement has taken to the streets in large numbers to vociferously denounce these killings and the race-based inequities in our legal system, including mass incarceration. They demand an end to these murders. They demand that the perpetrators be brought to justice, and that mechanisms like community control of the police be implemented to stop future abuses. Growing numbers of people are becoming aware that there is something seriously wrong with our judicial system, and for some, the entire system.

While this nascent movement is a necessary step toward ending racism, deepening the social, political and organizational orientation in this movement will increase chances for success. While most of these anti-racist and anti-police brutality movements are still single-issue campaigns, a growing number are being linked with other social justice movements. This is extremely important, and more linkages should be made. The next step is to go deeper to expose the roots of these racist and predatory practices in the capitalist system itself. As more people understand this at the street level and in the neighborhoods, the anti-racist movement and all other progressive movements will be stronger, broader, and will see that the struggle must be enlarged to fight for socialism.

Gains made on progressive single-issue campaigns are always subject to being rolled back if the super-structural institutions of society are not changed. We see today that right-wing extremist counter-insurgencies are intent on rolling back by 40-60 years civil rights gains, affirmative action, collective bargaining, and voting rights, victories won by the people in their hard-fought struggles. A key component in uprooting discriminatory practices is to uproot discriminatory ideas from people's consciousness. We must recognize that all forms of discrimination, all predatory practices, and all disparate inequities in society have their roots in capitalism. So, in addition to fighting racism, we need to fight against sexism, anti-worker and anti-labor actions, ageism, homophobia, anti-immigrant discrimination, climate injustice, and all others. When we show that capitalism is the cause of all these injustices, we show that all social justice movements have a common enemy. That will help link us together.

The exploitation and degradation of African Americans have been major weapons of capitalism since the first days of slavery in the American colonies. Since Blacks suffer the most, the capitalists tell white workers that they have it better so don't oppose the system. But where racism is the worst, white workers are also worse off than their white brothers and sisters elsewhere. In the southern states, the brutal systems of slavery and Jim Crow have severely lowered the wages and living standards for Black people, but also of southern whites compared to whites in the rest of the country.

Divide-and-conquer are time-tested tactics of capitalism to weaken both blacks and whites. Our response must be to build multi-racial unity, and unity with all who are exploited and oppressed. Spreading class consciousness and opposition to capitalism is critical. We can learn a lot from both the successes and mistakes of past movements. When these movements did not go to the root of the problem and failed to see that capitalism was its key cause, it was easier for the capitalists to derail them. For those who understood capitalism's role, these movements and individuals persevered. These anti-capitalists were not derailed from their mission, nor confused by new theories like neoliberalism. They knew that only by replacing capitalism with socialism could we begin to create a truly humane society.

When we build alliances there is strength in numbers. When I come to your aid to assist in your struggle, I win a fellow warrior for my own liberation. While there are different issues, there is only one righteous struggle - against all forms of discrimination, and for equality, justice, respect, and cooperation - ultimately, socialism.

Youth Marginalized by Capitalism

Capitalism has undergone some profound changes from my parents' generation to mine. Marx's description of capitalism, with its capitalist and working classes in conflict, holds true today. Marx also wrote about other groups, such as small individual and family-owned businesses, many of whom continue to be squeezed out of business by the large corporations. Then there is another group which has grown in size among my generation, and that is those who have been pushed out of the working class or were never able to get established in it because there aren't enough permanent jobs for everyone in this phase of capitalism's development, and decay. Marx called us the "Industrial Reserve Army," unemployed and under employed workers that could be pitted against employed workers over too few jobs. When industry closed manufacturing plants in the US in the late 1970s, 1980s and later, millions of workers lost their jobs, and many never found a comparable job. They unwillingly joined the Industrial Reserve Army.

Black Lives Matter protest in Los Angeles

My generation - their children, didn't have the option of getting those kinds of jobs because they were mostly gone by the time we grew up. Those jobs had been transferred overseas by capitalists to exploit poorly paid workers there. Part-time work, precarious work, the underground economy, mass and chronic unemployment have grown for all workers, but especially the youth of my generation, and even more among Black and Latino youth. That situation, combined with increasing mechanization in the US, and more jobs were lost. It's little wonder that many have given up hope for a better future. Many of these young people are now in prison.

Some in my generation went to college to get education for jobs in the "information" economy, but graduated to find "not hiring" signs. These young people, with tens of thousands of dollars in student debt and no job, were outraged. Many of them organized the Occupy Wall Street movement which correctly pointed the finger at Wall Street and capitalism as the cause of high and chronic unemployment and other injustices. While many in the Occupy movement are influenced by anarchism, I would suggest that getting to anarchism's goal of an egalitarian society without government and hierarchies would have a greater chance of success by going thru Marxism and socialism first.

Government Jobs Programs Needed

Privately owned capitalist businesses haven't provided the number of jobs needed to put the unemployed to work. If they create jobs it's because they expect to make a substantial profit on those workers' labor. If little profit is to be made, jobs aren't created. That's why we need the government to step in to create jobs, like the Works Progress Administration did during the capitalist-caused Great Depression and which put 8 million unemployed to work. And we need productive jobs that will help make life better for people, not the unproductive parasitic jobs that finance capitalism creates.

Look at a construction worker and a Wall Street financial derivatives trader. The construction worker produces things that people can use - a house, a hospital, a building where people work, roads and bridges. Everyone recognizes the contribution construction workers make to society. Unfortunately, the construction worker is not fully rewarded for his or her contributions since the employer takes a portion of the value the worker created. The construction worker may or may not live well, depending on how high or low his or her wage is, how many hours they work, how long they're out of work, the prices the worker must pay to live, if they have a union, and other factors.

The derivatives trader, on the other hand, produces nothing. Many get rich by betting against the success or failure of another person. A derivatives trader will sell someone's junk bonds or debt obligations that the trader thinks will tank, and when they do, the trader walks off with someone else's money. Under capitalism, this is not only legal, but rewarded. If the construction worker asks for a pay increase or joins a union to create a better life, they and their union are attacked as greedy and selfish. Truth is turned upside down.

Those of us who have been left out by this system want a new future. Prisoners want jobs when we get out of prison. There are 2.3 million people behind bars in the US. Even after we have served our time, we are discriminated against. It's very hard for former prisoners to get a job, we can't vote in many states, and many other doors are closed to us. The kinds of jobs we want and the training we need are for productive jobs. We aren't going to become Wall Street derivatives traders. What is ironic is that many prisoners, who are mostly poor and working-class and very often people of color, have gone to prison for petty crimes, while Wall Street hustlers have ripped off millions of dollars from others and rarely see the inside of a courtroom, no less a cell.

One would think that the sharp rise in incarceration rates, disproportionately of young Blacks and Latinos which began in the 1970s and 1980s and hasn't tapered off, was a result of increasing crime. Incarceration rose dramatically in the 1980s after President Reagan launched his so-called "war on drugs." This, in part, shows a correlation between rising crime rates and rising rates of incarceration. But that changed starting in the 1990s. Incarceration rates and prison construction continued to rise, while the rate of crime dropped. Very recently and very modestly the incarceration rate has tapered off somewhat, but the overall rate and number are still astronomical.

Youth of Color Criminalized

Crime is a social phenomenon resulting from negative social conditions, such as unemployment, poverty, abusive treatment, and others. In our society certain groups are criminalized - Black and Latino youth especially. We are targeted by police and the criminal justice system, and locked up at higher rates than other groups for similar behavior. Michelle Alexander's book, *The New Jim Crow*, documents this. Crime is also an ideological creation used to justify certain political and economic policies that have little to do with preventing crime and more to do with constructing a culture of fear, division, racism, and the prison industrial complex to keep the ruling elite in power.

The prison industry construction boom coincided with an era of rapidly rising and chronic unemployment. A major cause was the closings of major industrial factories, as mega-corporations packed up shop and moved overseas to take advantage of cheaper labor. When Ford, General Electric and other giants made this move, millions of workers lost their jobs. This deindustrialization allowed the capitalists to exploit cheaper labor abroad to increase profits, and to expand the "industrial reserve army" (unemployed people searching for work.) This allowed the capitalists to reduce wages. More unemployed workers looking for fewer jobs means more job competition, allowing employers to offer lower wages since someone will always be desperate enough to accept them. Then the more desperate-especially those still unemployed, turn to crime.

Then more prisons are built. Then more wars are launched, like against Iraq, to protect capitalism's overseas investments. The mass culture helped this process. The news media and entertainment industries like movies and TV programs are loaded with images of Black and Latino young people presented as thugs and criminals who should be locked up, or shot vigilante style on the street by the police. The ruling capitalist elite doubled down on its divide-and-conquer tactics by targeting especially the most down-trodden, those who had the least to lose by militant direct action.

Youth Need a Socialist Home

In this atmosphere the neo-liberal "tough on crime" agenda materialized into the juggernaut of coercive social control, not only for Black and Latino youth, but for everyone in the working-class. In 30-plus years, this has seriously weakened unionized workers' movements by slashing wages and benefits, rolling back civil rights gains, deregulating nearly everything, bludgeoning social programs, appropriating social wealth through an almost endless frenzy of austerity orgies, and locking up and disenfranchising nearly 2½ million people in our country. Another 5 million people have been relegated to the loss of democratic rights through the regressive laws governing ex-convicts through the restrictive parole and probation system.

Every year, approximately $70 billion is drained from state and federal coffers to maintain this industry to warehouse people (there is little or no rehabilitation, training, nor job placement for most inmates). This means much less money for education, health care, affordable housing, job creation programs. In impoverished urban neighborhoods and poor rural areas, young people have a better chance of going to prison than landing a living wage job. This is capitalism in deep crisis. Many young people think socialism is a better, more humane system, where meeting people's needs are put before enriching a small group of the very wealthy and powerful. Many young people may not know a lot of details about socialism, but many know that socialism means expanding democracy into all areas of life, so people - especially from the working-class, have more control over their lives. They understand that socialism means a society of cooperation and everyone looking out for each other.

But it's hard to work for socialism as an individual. In order to build this new society you have to work together with others. We can increase our knowledge and increase our effectiveness when we work together with other like-minded people in a socialist organization. I invite other young people to consider joining the Committees of Correspondence for Democracy and Socialism. It's an organization that fights for needed reforms today to help workers, people of color and the poor and marginalized in a way that helps us also fight for socialism. Members are encouraged to study and try different kinds of organizing to see what works best. It's important for the most oppressed and marginalized segments of the working-class, especially Blacks, Latinos and other people of color, young people, people from the LGBT community, the unemployed and the low paid workers, prisoners, and poor people to have a home, and that home should be in the organized socialist left. That is the road to take to stop the daily abuses and to improve our daily lives now, while we work to create the building blocks of a future socialist society.

Alex Krehbiel is an African American young man who is an inmate in a California prison and a member of CCDS.

Rage Against the Narrative: How To Understand Psychic Violence & Murder

By Lisa Brock

"The Whole Damn System is Guilty as Hell." Ferguson Protest Chant

"I don't do diversity, I do triage." Donte Hilliard, Former Asst. Dean & Director, Multicultural Student Center, University of Wisconsin, Madison

"To say Obama is progress is saying that he's the first Black person that is qualified to be president. That's not Black progress. That's white progress. There's [sic] been Black people qualified to be president for hundreds of years." Chris Rock, Comedian.

The uprising in Ferguson, Missouri, which has spread throughout the country in response to police and state violence against Black people, has proven cathartic to a disillusioned and weary populace. In the words of James Baldwin in his 1966 essay, "A Report from Occupied Territory," what was unleashed by Ferguson, was simply an overflow of the "unimaginably bitter cup." Every African American, almost to a person, has had unprovoked experiences with the police and a relationship in some way with a brutal and unjust Prison Industrial Complex. And every Black family and community has experienced violence, frame-ups, and/or unwarranted death at the hands of police and state agencies. African Americans and their allies of all strata, from youth to professional athletes to congressional aides and middle school children, are standing up because we need to; we have to. We have all been waiting for this moment to collectively speak this "truth to power".

Power, however, is not happy. Resistance is, after all, the ultimate challenge to the master narrative. It reveals for all to see the lies and contradictions in not only the master's actions but also its myths. According to Jean-François Lyotard, Master Narratives or Grand Narratives are the big stories, began during ancestral times that justify society and its power relations. The settlement of the pilgrims, the melting pot, manifest destiny, and capitalism are among the anchors of the US Grand Narrative. The historical plot of police as a benevolent institution that serves and protects is a meta-narrative. It is a story, among many, that supports the grand tale.

What might be called modern police emerged during the early 19th century largely in northern cities where the political party in power controlled the police forces. Hired and fired by mayors, police chiefs would order their men to engage in political campaigning and to harass political opponents. Police were also instructed to engage in social welfare for white citizens in order to maintain party loyalty and secure white male votes.

By the latter part of the 19th century, as Black and immigrant numbers increased in the cities, fighting street crime, preserving "social order," and protecting the property of the mercantile classes became the primary tasks of police forces. As Police Studies scholar Gary Potter has noted, "What constitutes social and public order depends largely on who is defining those terms." I would add to that, crime. Crime was largely defined as the petty theft and disturbances of the working classes.

In the South, securing property was also the goal. But Africans were that property. Slave patrols began in colonial America and were among America's first police forces. Their job was to apprehend runaway slaves, deliver brutal and often public punishment to those that challenged authority, and to put down slave resistance. As Sally E. Hadden has noted, "most law enforcement, was by definition, white patrolmen watching, catching or beating Black slaves." After the Civil War, the Ku Klux Klan and white vigilantes took over this role in an attempt to prevent Blacks from voting and exercising their 14th and 15th amendment rights.

As reconstituted Southern states "rose again" in the words of Jefferson Davis, the job of local police was largely to maintain white supremacy and segregation. They also "criminalized" Blacks through a corrupt system of fining and arrest for breaking trumped up laws such as spitting on the street or walking too close to white women. This was done to provide uncompensated labor for the convict lessee system, in which hundreds of thousands of Blacks were "sold" for a fee by local municipalities to farms and industries. White planters, the coal mining industry and US Steel benefitted tremendously from this labor force. According to the University of Houston's Digital History Library, nearly 73% of all revenue in Alabama in 1898 was generated from this system.

The meta-narrative of police today is built on these two legs. It is clear from Ferguson and beyond, that though much has changed, much has stayed the same.

Here are but three of many examples: First, it was discovered after the shooting of Mike Brown that Black Ferguson residents are gratuitously fined and arrested in order to fund the city coffers, making up 21% of the city's annual revenue. This is suspected to be the case in many poor municipalities today.

'Die-In' during Black Lives Matter protest in Kalamazoo, Michigan on December 5, 2014.

Second, "crime" continues to be construed in such a way that "breaking the law" is something primarily the poor and working classes do. Politicians, corporate bankers and government agents who declare war, engage in massive fraud and engage in torture are not characterized as criminals who should be arrested and jailed in the US. When I raised this contradiction with family members over the holiday, they laughed. "Not going to happen," they said.

Third, the brutal police response to the initial protest in Ferguson is clearly the result of the notion to maintain social order at all cost. It also exposed the highly militarized arsenal that local police now have at their disposal. Moreover, the near universal condemnation by the media to "looting" is connected to the reification of property and its protection.

Capitalism is an anchor in the Grand Narrative of the US, and a huge part of the meta-narrative of the police is to protect it. While the police are publicly touted as a force that fights crime and serves and protects, they are also a racist institution – whether they have officers of color or not – that regulates majority Black communities very much like they did during slavery and Jim Crow. In recent polls taken by newspapers such as the *Washington Post* and Gallup, it appears that most white Americans actually believe the meta-narrative of police serving and protecting all equally.

The Scary Black Thug

Yet, I would argue, if asked a slightly different question many would also say that the protection of citizens [largely raced white] from the criminal gangs and scary thugs [largely raced Black and brown] is a primary function of police as well.

What many Americans might not know is that the trope of the scary Black thug is simply that, a device born of politicians, Hollywood, record labels and the news media. Another meta-narrative so deeply constructed over the last thirty years that it has come to undermine a sense of common humanity across the racial chasm. White fear of the Black thug led to the killing of innocent youth such as Renisha McBride (Detroit suburb), who had a car break down, and Jonathan Ferrell (Charlotte, NC), who was in a car accident. Both were simply looking for help from white citizens.

George Zimmerman successfully deployed this trope in his defense of the murder of Trayvon Martin and so did Darren Wilson, the police officer in Ferguson who killed 18-year-old Mike Brown. Among other things, Wilson said this in his testimony to the grand jury: "when I grabbed him, the only way I can describe it is I felt like a 5-year-old holding onto Hulk Hogan...and he had the most intense aggressive face...it look[ed] like a demon." Sadly, these are just a few cases where white fear of the dangerous Black thug is a play in actual murder and legal defenses. Even more disturbing, though, is the fact so many juries believe it.[1]

On a relevant note: in a die-in in Kalamazoo, Michigan, on December 5, 2014, as nearly 400 people lay quietly on the ground, a man walks by and breaks the silence with this, "I support law enforcement because they keep me safe from thugs like you."

James Baldwin, in his *Nation* essay mentioned above, was writing about Harlem as the occupied territory that exploded in rebellion in 1964 for the exact same reason that Ferguson did in 2014. What Baldwin penned then could have been written today:

"This is why those pious calls to 'respect the law,' always to be heard from prominent citizens each time the ghetto explodes are so obscene. The law is meant to be my servant and not my master, still less my torturer and my murderer. To respect the law, in the context in which the American Negro finds himself, is simply to surrender his self-respect."

Notes

[1] This trope of the Black thug serves a similar function to the Black rapist of white women 100 years ago for which many Black people were lynched.

Lisa Brock is a Senior Editor and the Academic Director of the Arcus Center for Social Justice Leadership.

Police Violence, Capital & Neoliberalism

By Gary Potter

The nationwide movement against police violence and mass incarceration has brought to light the repressive and coercive nature of the criminal justice system in the United States. Attention has been focused on both the egregious disparities in incarceration between the US and other Western industrial states and a plethora of cases of lethal force used by the police against civilians.

These are vital issues. But given less attention is the issue of how we have arrived at such violent, coercive and repressive policies of social control in the United States. In this essay I will focus on neoliberalism and its impact on policing as a broader explanation of how we have become what Jock Young called a retributive society.

As defined by David Harvey, neoliberalism is "a theory of political economic practices that proposes that human well-being can best be advanced by liberating individual entrepreneurial freedoms and skills within an institutional framework characterized by strong private property rights, free markets, and free trade." Neoliberalism has resulted in a series of social changes that have fundamentally changed the nature and purpose of policing in the United States.

First, it has required new modes of spatial use, development and governance, particularly in urban areas. Second, it has created political, economic and social conditions which resulted in the invention of new crimes and new actuarial patterns of crime control. Third, neoliberalism requires an unprecedented and enormous expansion of the criminal justice system and concomitantly requires a more repressive and coercive criminal justice system.

The neoliberal state is committed to policies highly desired by and insisted upon by corporate and elite interests. The flip side of that coin is that neoliberalism fundamentally changes how the state deals with the poor, the unemployed, the underemployed and the homeless. Policing

follows suit with violent repression directed at the poor and virtual immunity extended to corporate, white-collar and political criminals.

Central to neoliberal policies have been rapid and massive changes in the spatial and socioeconomic characteristics of cities. Neighborhoods have experienced rapacious acquisition of properties by realtors and developers, resulting in skyrocketing rents and rapid gentrification. As the federal, state and city governments withdrew support from social programs and services local communities experienced unprecedented levels of unemployment, underemployment, poverty, homelessness and social crime, the profits from which helped to fill the voids created by a declining economy. At the same time the privileged, realtors, developers, businesses and banks experienced a massive increase in wealth at the expense of the vast majority of urban residents.

The impact of neoliberalism in relation to rental housing costs is obvious and draconian:

Median Rents Unfurnished Apartments U.S.

Year	Median Rent
1980	$308
1990	$600
2000	$841
2010	$1,077
2014	$1,314

That's an over 400% increase in rental housing costs between 1980 and 2014. At the same time the median household income in 1990 was $49,950 increasing to only $50,054 in 2011 (U.S. Census Bureau) an increase of 1%. Combine that fact with a U.S. poverty rate exceeding 15% in 2011 and the devastating impact of gentrification becomes painfully obvious. *Source:http://www.statista.com/statistics/200223/median-apartment-rent-in-the-us-since-1980/*

Concomitantly more and more urban public space, like parks and recreation areas were privatized. Now open spaces were under corporate financial control and those areas were subjected to draconian levels of police intervention. The banks and corporations did not want people singing, drinking, playing, or sleeping in those suddenly private places.

All of these things became criminal acts and all of these things became priorities for a new corporatized American police force which no longer owed any allegiance to the people but only to private capital.

Starting with the Reagan administration the federal government began to cease investment in urban renewal programs and urban development. Funds which had been made available to local city governments dried up and disappeared.

The withdrawal of federal support had two main impacts. First, a wide range of positive social and development programs were terminated. Second, cities faced a problem of rapidly increasing debt. With the federal government's retreat from governance to sovereignty, urban governments increasingly looked to banks and financiers to cover their costs and obligations.

The banks were only too happy to fill the void. They predicated their underwriting of municipal governance with three demands. First, social welfare programs had to be ravaged. Second, municipal services and space had to be privatized. Third, order maintenance through aggressive policing had to serve the interests of land developers, realtors, banks, corporations and private business. In other words, municipal government had to divest itself from its own populace and as a result the police no longer served the community - they served finance capital alone.

So, municipal governments no longer governed. They became profit-producing, entrepreneurial, sovereign fiefdoms no longer serving their residents but totally focused on policies that made urban areas financially, socially and politically attractive to corporations, developers and banks. A combination of private and corporate financial investment and urban government policies created the conditions for a perfect storm of gentrification that deliberately displaced impoverished neighborhoods, massively widened wealth differentials, exacerbated class conflicts and required a militarized, violent army of occupation. Gentrification turned police departments into privately-owned, violent, security forces who no longer answered to the people they allegedly served.

New Crime and Actuarial Policing

The simple fact is that almost everyone's contact with the criminal justice system starts with the police. In fact, the overwhelming majority of Americans will have interactions with the police as their only criminal justice system contact. These interactions rarely result in arrest, let alone prosecution conviction or incarceration. In fact, of all those people who have been subjected to "stop and frisk" police tactics, 90% are never found to be engaged in criminal activity. That fact alone demonstrates that the police are not fighting crime but are engaged in a pattern of discipline and regulation directed at those targeted by neoliberal policies. The police are not protecting communities and keeping them secure; the police are playing a key role in destabilizing and reshaping those communities for the benefit of financial entrepreneurs.

Beginning in the 1990s many police departments abandoned "crime-fighting" in favor of an "order maintenance" policing strategy. Rather than targeting serious crimes like assault, robbery, rape, burglary, theft and homicide, police departments turned their attention to minor, low-level instances of "disorder." So incivility and behavior which is somehow defined as annoying like homelessness, panhandling, public alcohol consumption and minor vandalism became the new "index crimes" targeted by police departments. The result was obvious. The police engaged in punitive, oppressive and often violent tactics directed primarily at poor, inner-city communities. The net impact was that policing was no longer directed at serious crime, it was the new social engineering policy of the state to attack poverty.

The neoliberal demand for order maintenance makes a mockery of arguments that policing strategies are designed to protect us from harm from violent and property crimes. In 2013 police made 11,302,102 arrests. Of those 480,360 (4%) were for violent crimes and 1,559,284 (13.8%) were for property crimes. In view of the simple fact that arrest is the starting point for most police violence against civilians the question becomes what exactly is the police doing that require so many other arrests? The answer is that they were engaged in policing disorder, rudeness and bothersome behavior not crime.

The most telling category of arrests is the amorphous category of "all other offenses", defined by the FBI as "all violations of state or local laws not specifically identified as Part I or Part II offenses, except traffic violations." In other words all criminal acts not defined by the FBI as being "serious" crimes. In 2013 police made 3,282,651 (29%) arrests for "all other" infractions, a number dwarfing arrests for both violent and property offenses. But, it's worse than that. In addition to the "all other offenses" category police made 1,441,209 arrests (12.8% of all arrests) for vandalism, curfew violation and loitering, vagrancy, disorderly conduct, drunkenness and liquor law violations (excluding drunk driving), extremely minor offenses as well. So 42% of police arrests were for public order indiscretions. If we add to those numbers the victimless crimes of prostitution and drug abuse (1,549,663 arrests and 13.7% of all arrests) we end up with a total 56% of all arrests that posed no discernible threat to the public.

Punitive Policing Is All About Power

Punitive policing has nothing to do with crime. It is, in fact, a symbolic representation of state power, a form of public humiliation and public punishment. Order maintenance strategies were directed almost exclusively against the poor and people of color in the United States. Policing became the primary tool of neoliberalism to control, humiliate and regulate the poor.

New crimes and new policing strategies like those associated with Wilson and Kelling's infamous "Broken Windows Theory" had very little to do with serious crime. Instead, a plethora of new laws and policing priorities were focused on one thing and one thing only, the protection of capital flows to protect and enhance private investment and development in urban settings. For example, one of the first campaigns launched by New York Police Department (NYPD) under its "broken windows" paradigm was to crack down on and arrest street vendors. It was, of course, just this type of policing strategy that led to the tragic police-killing of Eric Garner in Staten Island, New York City, for selling cigarettes on the streets. The demand for new laws and aggressive policing of street life came directly from commercial interests who argued that street vending, street artists, and the like created congestion on sidewalks and competed with the products being peddled in their stores. Aggressive policing toward sidewalk vendors, singers, dancers and artists had nothing to do with serious crime. It had everything to with private profit.

Tool For Gentrification

Similarly, it was corporate real estate developers who pushed for aggressive policing and changes in police deployment strategies as a means to clear out neighborhoods for gentrification. Once again new laws and aggressive policing strategies were aimed at the homeless, the poor and the mentally ill. Corporate elites wielded their considerable political clout to reallocate police resources from "crime" to removing obstacles to their takeover of land and buildings and their subsequent profits from skyrocketing rents and sales of refurbished urban housing. Simply put, the police were used to displace entire populations and sanitize the streets not for the benefit of residents, but for the profits of corporations.

NYPD's Compstat program is the prime example of how police resources are reallocated for private profit. New York's police commissioner Bill Bratton was a primary architect of this new form of police accountability to corporate interests. Bratton reorganized the NYPD around "private-sector business practices and principles for management." Compstat, in addition to heightening police accountability to financial capital also decreased police accountability to poor communities. No longer were the concerns of residents the primary motivation for police activity. Now the police were accountable only to actuarial statistical patterns and numbers which served to define "disorder" in a manner conducive to private business and development. Compstat in no way provided any meaningful community input to policing. It was and is a total rejection of community input and the full embrace of private business and financial section input.

The result of all of this was the criminalization of "disorder." Suddenly police became more concerned about panhandling, public singing and dancing, loitering, public drinking, bicycle riders, boom boxes, prostitutes, graffiti and street vending than they were about serious criminal harms. Criminalizing previously noncriminal acts resulted in a strategy of order-maintenance policing that was both punitive and judgmental in vilifying those who might be marginally annoying but in no way dangerous. This was both a gift to corporate interests and a war on the poor. In concert with the severe cuts to social service programs and the new definition of "crime" as disorder, policing became a major policy initiative in dealing with structural poverty.

Criminal Expansion

Neoliberal policies including massive corporate tax cuts and even corporate tax forgiveness along with the gutting of the progressive income tax, created levels of inequality in the United States unheard of since slavery and the rise of the robber barons. The redistribution of income alone was astonishing. In 1980 the top 10% of income earners controlled 35% of all income. Today they control more than 50%. The Gini Ratio which measures income inequality soared to .46 making the United States the most unequal industrialized country in the world.

At the same the US prison population soared from around 500,000 in 1980 to over 2.5 million today with another 5 million under the control of one or another correctional programs. Today the United States has the highest rate of incarceration in the world and one out of every 30 adults are under control of the correctional system. And all this occurred in the midst of a dramatic drop in criminal victimization. The violent crime rate in 1981 was 52.3 per 1,000 people. In 2013 it was 26.1 per 1,000 people. The rise in incarceration had nothing to with crime. It had everything to do with an orderly corporatized society.

Neoliberalism has adopted a policy of incarceration as a response to control of poor communities and a growing surplus population of the unemployed and underemployed. As neoliberal policies have abandoned the state's function of governance and eviscerated welfare policies it has looked to the criminal justice system as its primary response to poverty. That response has included both punitive and aggressive policing and the vindictive use of incarceration. The disorderly among us are subjected to arrest, police violence, incarceration and displacement from their communities. Order maintenance policing (Broken Windows) targets the homeless, the mentally ill and the poor for arrest and prosecution.

Purpose of 'Stop and Frisk'

Police resources are disproportionately reassigned to poor communities. A massive 33% nationwide cut in spending on health care for the mentally ill, including funds for medication, has resulted in police intervention as a primary modality to deal with psychiatric problems. Once the concept of crime was replaced by quality-of-life violations of local ordinances, it was easy for police to find "cause" to stop-and-frisk almost anyone. Despite the fact that stop-and-frisk policies rarely resulted in arrests or the discovery of actual "crime", nonwhites were subjected to the tactic six times more frequently than Caucasians even with crime rates held constant. In New York City 90% of the precincts with high frequencies of police stops were majority-minority precincts. Analyzes of stops found that the strongest predictive variable was the poverty rates of the neighborhoods in which the stops occurred.

Conclusion

Broken windows policing and the neoliberal policies on which it is based represent a policy of vilification of the poor. The very act of being stopped, even if there is no arrest constitutes punishment. It is an invasion of privacy, it is public humiliation, and it is a denial of liberty. Neoliberalism has resulted in punitive, order maintenance policing which is nothing more than the symbolic assertion of state coercion and violence. It is a spectacle created to assert state power and discipline in the service of private capital.

References

Center on Race, Crime and Justice. 2010. Stop, question & frisk policing practices in New York City. John Jay College of Criminal Justice.

Gilmore, R. 2007. Prisons, surplus, crisis, and opposition in globalizing California. University of California Press.

Hackworth, J. 2006. The neoliberal city: Governance, ideology, and development in American urbanism. Cornell University Press.

Gary Potter is a professor of Criminal Justice and Police Studies at Eastern Kentucky University

Color Blindness in the Age of Escalating Racism

By Ted Pearson

(Editors' note: Rahm Emanual, corporate candidate for mayor of Chicago, recently defeated the progressive candidate, Jesus "Chuy" Garcia, and even won many election wards that had a Black majority of voters. Several commentators have stated that the Garcia campaign fatally avoided the most pressing concerns of the Black community. Ted Pearson takes to task the election analyses by several progressive writers for what they missed.)

The three analyses of the Chicago Mayoral election by Amisha Patel, John Nichols and Thomas A. Corfman (Portside April 9, 2015) are remarkable mainly for what they don't say. They accurately describe the coalition around the progressive candidate, Jesus "Chuy" Garcia, as grassroots, including very important large industrial unions such as the Teachers, Transit Workers, and Service Employees. They note the historic quality of this coalition. But by their omissions they endanger the very coalition they are proclaiming.

Throughout the election campaign, and in these analyses, you would never know that Chicago is a city in which over half the population suffers under virtual military occupation. If you only listened to the pundits and the candidates, you would never know that:

• Chicago has a rate of racial profiling and "stop and frisk" incidents by police that far exceeds that of any other city in the country, including New York, according to a study by the ACLU.
• Since 2007 in Chicago 121 people have been murdered by Chicago police, and that 93 per cent have been people of color. That's the official count; the actual number is thought to be much higher.
• Cook County Jail is the largest prison or jail in the country, and 85 per cent of the inmates are Black or Latino.

• The Chicago Police have been exposed as maintaining a secret torture center on the West Side, where suspects are kept incommunicado, off the books and out of sight by anyone except the police, and where at least one suspect has died.

You would also never know that there have been mass protests all over the country, including Chicago, by Black, Latino and white people, mainly youth, demanding justice and an end to police crimes.

Only Nichols even mentions race, and that is in a wistfully recalled quotation from the late Mayor Harold Washington: "We are a multi-ethnic, multi-racial, multi-language city and that is a source of stability and strength." In his first campaign, Nichols notes, "Washington simply had to pull together a coalition of African-Americans, Latinos and liberal reformers. But it didn't happen [in 1977]." It did happen in 1983, when Washington won election. It didn't happen in Chicago in 2015, however, only this time no one even talks about it.

It is not enough to observe (as none of these observers did) that such a Washington coalition did not emerge in the most recent election. It is more important to observe that the progressive coalition in this election and these liberal observers act as if there was no issue of white supremacy and racism in Chicago at all. It's the classic unmentioned elephant in the room.

The White Blindspot

Is this just accidental blindness, or is it a conscious refusal to talk about the single most important issue that prevents a solid coalition of progressive forces from emerging in this city? No one can know what goes on in the minds of these deep thinkers. But I am beginning to think that it's a willful refusal to deal with reality more than an inability to see. But why?

At least one leader of this movement, when confronted with the horrors of the police violence that is wreaking havoc among families in the city's Black and Latino communities, and the nation-wide mass upsurge against it led by the youth, responded that "these people don't vote, but white people do." The meaning was clear – white people can't understand this issue, and to raise it jeopardizes the progressive coalition.

This is not only morally bankrupt. It is historically wrong. The fight against racism has motivated people of all colors, including white people, in the US many times. This fight was at the heart of every progressive advance, whether it was the defeat of the old slavocracy in 1865, the defeat of Nazi Germany in 1945, the defeat of Jim Crow in 1965, the election of Harold Washington in 1983, or the defeat of apartheid in 1991, to name just a few of these historic victories. Black people and the struggle against the oppression of Black people, led by Black people, played the most important role in the United States in all these victories. The failure to recognize this historic reality has been, and will always be, the Achilles heel of the progressive movement in our country.

The election of Harold Washington in 1983 was first of all a rejection of the racist policies and arrogance of the incumbent Mayor Jane Byrne and her "regular" Democratic Party challenger, Richard M. Daley. It was mainly a campaign against racism, which was skillfully organized as a campaign for basic fairness by Harold Washington. This was something that united the Black community first and foremost, and won over majorities of Latinos and progressive whites. It was championed by the Left, which understood the centrality of the struggle for Black freedom in the United States. But this was missing in the 2015 campaign, even though the level of racism and racist repression in the city has grown since the untimely death of Mayor Washington in 1987.

Marx said that history repeats itself, the first as tragedy, then as farce. When will those of us who are not Black ever learn?

References

Amisha Patel, "Emanuel won the mayor's race, but progressives won the election," Crain's Chicago Business, April 8, 2015; John Nichols, "Chicago's Chuy Garcia Lost an Election, but Won a Movement," The Nation Blog, April 8, 2015; Thomas A. Corfman, "How Chicago's wealthiest neighborhoods tipped the election to Emanuel," Crain's Chicago Business, April 8, 2015.

David Moberg, "Chicago Progressives' Mixed Results Against the 'Money Machine'," In These Times, April 10, 2015. Moberg does discuss the Washington coalition and the ability of Mayor Rahm Emanuel to defuse the massive anger in the Black community. The endorsement of Emanuel by President Obama and robo-calls to Black voters were responsible, Moberg says. They certainly were a factor. However, Moberg, like the others, completely misses the contemporary repression of Black people by the police and the refusal of so many progressives, including Jesus Garcia, to take this up. Moberg also doesn't appear to understand that it was mass anger against racist oppression by the old Democratic Machine was what generated the unity of the Black community in 1983, making the election of Harold Washington possible.

Ted Pearson is a member of the National Alliance Against Racist and Political Repression.

Digna And Me: Cuba, Race And Transnational Solidarity

By Lisa Brock

(Editorial Note: On December 14, 2014, President Obama announced to great excitement that he planned to modify the 55-year-old US blockade against Cuba. Given that Congress passed major pieces of the embargo law, Obama is limited in what he can do. Yet, a robust set of negotiations has begun. Lisa Brock recently returned from Cuba, where there is both excitement at the possibilities of open ties with the US, and concern over Obama's hostile turn towards Venezuela, Cuba's strongest ally. Interestingly, many of Brock's US-based colleagues have asked her, did you see changes as a result of the US turn toward normalization? Brock's answer is this: Cuba is always changing and has been shifting towards a mixed economy for years. Normalizing relations with the US is just the latest move in this direction. As Tom Hayden wrote in The Democracy Journal,[1] it is not Cuba that has been stuck and isolated but the US. Brock, for one, has been writing about and engaging in solidarity with Cuba for 25 years.)

Last summer (2014), my friend, colleague and "hermana" Dr. Digna Castañeda Fuertes spent three months with me, here in the US. Digna is a 78-year-old Cuban woman and is the first Black professor emeritus in the 285-year-old history of the University of Havana. While this may at first seem dumbfounding, it shouldn't. Harvard University, founded in 1636, did not grant emeriti status to an African-American until 1999, which was during its 363rd year. Slavery and racism prevented Blacks from employment and status at most predominantly white institutions of higher education throughout the Americas until the 1960s. For US Blacks, increased opportunities in higher education are due to the Civil Rights Movement. For Blacks in Cuba, it has been the result of the Cuban revolution.

Digna spent last summer with me because I am writing a biography of her. My desire to do this biography came about after an interview I did of Cuban filmmaker Gloria Rolando Casamayor for a British publication. It struck me that Gloria and Digna are not just Cuban collaborators with whom I have worked in solidarity for nearly twenty-five years. These two extraordinary women are the Cuban revolution. They were among the cohorts of young people who made the revolution, benefitted from it, still believe in it and are struggling to make it better.

Digna and Lisa, Summer 2014

Digna was twenty-two years old and a first year university student when the revolution triumphed in 1959. She remembers quite well that she and her parents struggled to pay that first year's tuition. After the revolution, attending university was free. She remembers the cruelty of the Batista regime and how her father, known as the best tamale maker in Havana, suffered its indignities. She also remembers Fidel coming to her university at night to talk to students about the brave new world ahead. She was completely swept up by the promise of the revolution.

Like all university students at the time, Digna was charged with both studying and teaching. She taught secondary students by day, attended university classes at night, and on the weekends she worked with the youth who had returned from Cuba's now famed National Literacy Campaign. In 1961, over 250,000 people participated in Cuba's massive effort to end illiteracy in Cuba. They taught more than 707,000 other Cubans, most of them rural, to read and write. Almost half of these volunteer teachers were under 18 and more than half were women. Digna and her cohort taught these young people when they returned to Havana, so that they could continue to advance their own education. In 1959, Cuba had about a 60% literacy rate. By the end of 1961, it was at 96%. Today, Cuba claims one of the most literate populations of the world.[2] Digna said: "While I was running all over Havana and up all night with friends and comrades, those early days of the revolution were the best days of my life."

Comparative Race Analysis and Transnational Solidarity

Digna, and I first met in 1990 during an academic exchange organized by the University of Havana and the US-based Radical Philosophy Association. Otis Cunningham and I were publishing a long review essay in Cuban Studies on Carlos Moore's controversial 1988 book, *Castro, the Blacks and Africa*, and were on a panel with Digna, who served as a respondent to our piece. Moore's book had created a big stir in both the US and Cuba because it argued that the socialist revolution of Cuba, and Fidel Castro, himself, were racist. Digna was an established scholar at the time and I was an emerging scholar-activist. Our panel opened up in a lively and hot conversation on comparative "race and racism" in the US and Cuba.

My colleague, Otis, and I argued that while Moore's attack on the Cuban revolution was poorly researched and clearly unsubstantiated, it nonetheless gained wide readership because there had been so little written about race in Cuba since 1959. Digna, like many Cubans at the time, disagreed with us, arguing that racism was no longer a problem in Cuba. The revolution, at the time, held that racism was the result of economic and structural inequalities and that because those had been eradicated, racism in Cuba had withered away. While it was clear that the Cuban revolution had upended society's systemic barriers to equality by guaranteeing free or nearly free housing, education, healthcare, and food for all, we still felt that without research and discourse, there was no way to prove or disprove a continuation of racist ideologies and cultural forms in Cuba.

In fact, we felt that Moore had written the book with an US Black audience in mind, with the aim of distancing us from any solidarity we might cultivate with Cuba. His language and his critique pushed our particular buttons. He argued that Black Cubans lacked race pride and that many continued to be called mulattos. This of course was done without any attention to the fact that the tri-racial identification system of Black, mulatto and white was common all over Latin America.

Even more curious was the fact that he talked about Cuba's role in Africa as being hated by Africans, which was simply not true. Cuba had played a key role in defeating the apartheid forces in Angola, which led to the independence of Namibia and was part of what ultimately led to Mandela's release and the end of the apartheid regime in South Africa. [3] Yet, without counter narratives on the state of race and racism in Cuba, and with a cynical US Black population, we worried that Moore's work was gaining traction.

Digna and her cohorts pushed back at that conference. While they applauded our Civil Rights and Black Power movements, they thought our focus on race was problematic. Cuba and the US were totally different, they argued, and Moore's critiques were so off base that they did not deserve a response. After all, Cubans had not only liberated their country from the grips of US imperialism but were supporting African freedom movements and teaching tens of thousands of African students in Cuba. Black Cubans had also maintained their connection to African spiritual practice, through Santeria, Palo Monte, and other African-based religions in a way that had been largely lost in the US. The question then was nicely posed to Otis Cunningham and I, what have you done in the

US? You have a lot of pride but no real power. We had to agree.

Cuban Intellectuals, 2015

What began at that conference continued throughout the 1990s at engagements there and exchanges here. It was a wonderful laboratory for comparative race analysis in the Americas and we developed a rich transnational solidarity in the process. We worried together over questions of race on two levels. How do we compare and contrast the social construction of race in Cuba and the US, on the one hand, and how does racism and resistance to it manifest differently in capitalist and socialist systems. Yet, a third level has always also been present. What do socialism and the struggle against racism look like under the pressure of an ever-present hostile world power like the US and how might it look different without such pressure?

Race in Cuba Today

The discourse on race in Cuba has changed dramatically since these early days. Digna as well as most Cubans of African descent, and even Fidel Castro, now admit that they overestimated the power of systemic change to alter, in Marxist terms, "the super-structure" of racism. A lack of Black representation in the curriculum and the media, along with the continuation of popular racist "stereotypical" images, exists in Cuba today. The decades-old lacunae on racial discourse in Cuba have led indeed to a reproduction of notions of white supremacy.

In the words of Dr. Esteban Morales, a leading sociologist and economist at the University of Havana:

"Despite the radical nature of the process that got underway in 1959, the country's social policies failed to take skin color into account. In terms of social policy, after the triumph of the revolution, all poor people were treated equally, without differentiating between whites and Blacks. But this was something that needed to be done, because the color of one's skin in Cuba is a significant variable in social differences.

"Despite the fact that everyone's living standards improved and Black Cubans achieved a more favorable position over the last half-century, the profound differences did not disappear entirely. During the special period (the economic crisis of the 1990s, following the collapse of the East European socialist bloc, we realized that those who were hit hardest by the crisis were in fact Black Cubans, who had fewer possibilities of forging a livelihood.

"Even in Cuba today, being poor and white is not the same as being poor and Black."

Morales and other Black intellectuals, while believers in the Cuban model, have been meeting to address the issue of race in Cuba today. In 2012, he, along with others, created the Aponte Commission to Combat Racism and Racial Discrimination in Cuba. 2012 marked the 200th anniversary of the 1812 José Aponte Black-led rebellion in Cuba and was a good moment to launch such a project. 2012 also marked the 100th anniversary of Cuba's Independent Party of Color, whose supporters were massacred (by Cuban elites and under US pressure) in 1912 after a popular uprising. Gloria Rolando released her documentary entitled Breaking the Silence on this history, which had until 2012 been largely ignored (or denied) in Cuba.

Black Cubans have also linked their current discussions of race to the UN's Resolution 68/237 which proclaimed 2015-2024 as the International Decade for People of African Descent, citing the need to strengthen national, regional and international cooperation in relation to the full enjoyment of economic, social, cultural, civil and political rights by people of African descent, and their full and equal participation in all aspects of society.[4] We here in the US have yet to really acknowledge this decade, even though the We Charge Genocide and Black Lives Matter movements are gaining increased international attention. What a remarkable opportunity that should not be missed.

Transnational solidarity is not blindly supporting those with whom we work, but joining together in a studied, yet politically sophisticated way, to critically engage each other on issues of social justice, so that we all learn and grow in the process. This is the only way to make a better world.

Notes

[1] "Why the US-Cuba Deal Really Is a Victory for the Cuban Revolution" by Tom Hayden
[2] See Catherine Murphy's award-winning documentary, Maestra, which is about this highly successful campaign.
[3] It would be like now, with the Ebola crisis, if someone was to publish a piece arguing that West Africans did not like Cuba sending hundreds of doctors to fight Ebola, because it is racist. It did not make sense. On his first international tour abroad, Nelson Mandela went to Cuba, visited Fidel Castro and thanked the people of Cuba for their support.
[4] 2015-2024 International Decade for People of African Descent website

Lisa Brock is a Senior Editor and the Academic Director of the Arcus Center for Social Justice Leadership in Michigan.

The Coercive State in Contemporary Capitalism:

Police killings, mass incarceration, anti-immigrant violence, pervasive surveillance, the ideology of criminality and what to do about it

By Jim Grant, Daniel Mejia and Zach Robinson

Alarming headlines announce the murders of Walter Scott and little Tamir Rice, lifeless bodies of children washing up on the banks of the Rio Grande, the quadrupling of the nation's prison population since the early 1970s, and the revelations by Julian Assange and Edward Snowden, now living in exile. Opinion polls show that Americans—stimulated by innumerable TV crime shows and sensationalist news reports—are "fed up with crime" and "paralyzed with fear." Yet the stirrings of social resistance suggest that these stories must be treated as part of a systemic whole. We choose the title of this article as much to be a stimulus to thought and action as it is a summary of the present short outline.

Our goal is to define, and sketch the foundations of, a systemic perspective that in our view ought to be more prominent in the movement today. This perspective, and the underlying reality, is undeniably grim. Although the brunt of the repression is borne by African-Americans, Latinos and Arab-Americans—and in different ways—the systemic nature of this complex of problems shows that each group is not alone and that white skin won't save you if you're a worker. Thus the systemic perspective is a unifying point of view, and as such, leaves us with a certain kind of optimism. Furthermore, it can lead to the formulation of programmatic goals in the movement that point beyond immediate struggles for remedies such as body cams and reform in police training.

This piece came out of discussions of the CCDS Task Force on Police and the State that the authors have led over the past several months; we consider the piece a work-in-progress. Task Force discussions began with a presentation by Frank Chapman of Chicago's National Alliance Against Racist and Political Repression about the movement to establish a greater measure of civilian control over the notorious Chicago Police through the struggle for a Civilian Police Accountability Council. We wish to thank all the members of the Task Force for stimulating discussions and the opportunity to develop our ideas.

I. The Homeland Security State.

The recent killings by police—brutal acts that have sparked a vibrant resistance movement—are tied together with mass incarceration, anti-immigrant violence on our borders, and surveillance as key aspects of the functioning of the ever-expanding Homeland Security state under the conditions of contemporary capitalism. It is remarkable how the existence of such a large machine remains, for the most part, out of the public eye.

But it is enough to think carefully about the so-called "War on Drugs" to see these gears mesh together in terrible synchrony. The recent resignation of the chief of the U.S. Drug Enforcement Administration (DEA), Michele Leonhart, amidst a furor over revelations that DEA agents in Colombia attended sex parties funded by drug cartels, speaks volumes. The drug cartels occupy a twilight zone between ally and foe, a case in point being former de facto Panamanian head-of-state Manuel Noriega, who was a long-time contractual operative of the CIA. Noriega's role in the drug trade was long known in Washington, and was certainly known by June, 1986, when Seymour Hersh reported on it in the New York Times. But he continued to make himself useful, aiding the U.S.-backed Contra war against the Sandinista government of Nicaragua. After the political pressure generated by the 1986 Iran-Contra revelations and the 1988 Kerry report, Noriega's refusal to allow Washington's man Guillermo Endara to be elected president on the eve of the first phase of

the transfer of the Panama canal to Panamanian control changed Washington's approach. The United States mounted an invasion of Panama in December, 1989, swore Endara in as President on a U.S. military base, and captured Noriega, who was then convicted of narcotics offenses in a Florida court. Two of the four official reasons given by President Bush for the invasion were "to protect the integrity of the Panama Canal Treaty" and "to combat drug trafficking." Under President Endara, however, the drug trade in Panama flourished as never before. The idea that combating drug trafficking is the primary mission of the War on Drugs is simply not credible.

According to the ACLU, the United States' 40-year-long War on Drugs has sent millions to prison for low-level offenses: "Mandatory minimum requirements have stripped judges of their ability to make the sentence fit the crime or the defendant, particularly when it comes to minimums for federal and state drug laws, which can require sentences of 20 years, 30 years, or even life for low-level dealers and addicts. The result has been that hundreds of thousands of people are serving decades-long, and in many cases mandatory, prison sentences that are far out of proportion to their crimes or culpability." The War on Drugs has had an intensifying effect on policing and police violence, both in the interior and on the border, that corresponds to its effect on the U.S. criminal justice system.

A 2000 study on "crime, punishment and public opinion" by The Sentencing Project identifies a huge gulf between reality and the public perception of crime. Unsurprisingly, it found that public opinion shifts in relation to political initiatives. And it is not hard to find negative initiatives. Coded into the HTML of the Fox News U.S. Crime web page descriptor is the phrase "Crime, murder, illegal drugs, missing kids, illegal aliens—FOXNews.com. Crime headlines. Latest on murder, illegal drugs and missing kids cases." It is indicative of the ideological word salad that is electronically force-fed to the public. And Michael Moore's *Bowling for Columbine* explores some of the cancerous effects of manufactured fear upon our society.

The Homeland Security State is a multi-faceted machine for dominance. The writings of Italian Marxist Antonio Gramsci help us to set it in the context of capitalism today. E. Collin Ruggero has a useful synopsis on his blog:

Gramsci theorized that dominant groups maintain their position through a mix of sheer force (coercion through political society) and, more importantly, with the active participation of the subordinate groups (consent through hegemony in civil society). The use of coercion in the process of domination is the domain of what he calls 'political society,' meaning "the armed forces, police, law courts and prisons, together with all the administrative departments concerning taxation finance, trade, industry, social security, etc." (Simon, 1990:71). In Gramsci's view, however, these are only a portion of the state's domination framework. Indeed, the role of political society, the "apparatus of state coercive power," is to enforce "discipline on those groups who do not 'consent'" (Gramsci, 2003:12). The state, or dominant group, only turns to coercive tactics if efforts to manufacture consent fail. Consent to domination, the second portion of Gramsci's formula of power, is developed within civil society. It is an internalized form of domination that differs from the external, "direct domination" achieved through the coercive force of political society (Gramsci, 2003:12). Civil society is the sphere within which the state pursues (and maintains) hegemony, a social order where "a common social-moral language is spoken, in which one concept of reality is dominant, informing with its spirit all modes of thought and behaviour" (Femia, 1981:24).

Hegemony, however, is not simply achieved through the alignment of the free choices of subordinate groups. Consent is actively manufactured within civil society; hegemony is pursued through "extremely complex mediums, diverse institutions, and constantly changing processes" (Buttigieg, 1995:7). "Through their presence and participation in various institutions, cultural activities, and many other forms of social interaction, the dominant classes 'lead' the society in certain directions" (Buttigieg, 2005:44). Hegemony operates through the social institutions of civil society: the church, the educational system, the press, all the bodies which help create in people certain modes of behaviour and expectations consistent with the hegemonic social order. Gramsci's civil society "is best described not as the sphere of freedom but of hegemony" (Buttigieg, 1995:6).

Thus, in Gramsci's terms, what we have been witnessing over the last 40 years, the period called out by the ACLU, is a shift in tactics toward more extensive methods of coercion by the ruling class.

Coercion is a historically documented response by capitalism to crises grave enough to threaten bourgeois social leadership or bourgeois property. Why it has taken the particular form it has in the United States today is almost certainly a matter of the nation's history as a European colonial settler state, one of the pillars of which was the institution of chattel slavery. The frontier outposts, slave patrols, chain gangs and Southern military schools were features of a society that has long cultivated a variety of means of intense repression, kept hidden in plain view behind a veil of racist ideology and national myth.

The Homeland Security State of today is also an outgrowth and a complement in domestic affairs to the National Security State that arose during the international conflicts of the First Cold War (and with the recent crisis in the Ukraine and the U.S. "Pivot to Asia," we are witnessing the deliberate provocation of a Second Cold War.) The domestic and international aspects of the coercive state are linked in the so-called "Global War on Terror," in the extensive program of arms transfer from the Pentagon to local police departments, and in myriad other ways.

The shift toward a more coercive state has a counterpart in the world of business. Economists Sam Bowles and Arjun Jayadev have extensively studied what they term the Guard Economy, that burgeoning sector of contemporary capitalism that produces nothing itself, and serves only to keep the rest of us in line. They point out that there are more Americans employed today as security guards than as high school teachers, one measure of the vast waste that follows in the wake of our dying economic order. In some measures of the extent of the Guard Economy, Bowles and Jayadev consider prisoners, along with their captors, as guards, in the sense that incarceration of a portion of the working class plays a role in disciplining the entire class. It is an analysis similar to Marx's point that the main functional role of capitalism's "reserve army of the unemployed" is to exert a downward pressure on wages. Today, apparently, the bourgeoisie does not consider unemployment to be a sufficient deterrent to working class aspirations.

To assess the state of civil rights and civil liberties, one must know what lies at the root of the capitalist shift toward substantially higher levels of coercion. The last 40 year period has been a time of growing crises that are closely tied to the way that capitalist production is structured. The dramatic graphs at Catherine Mulbrandon's blog VisualizingEconomics.com illustrate the story of economic stagnation in the United States: "Over the last couple of centuries there has been a steady increase in wages for both unskilled workers and production workers. A lot of this growth is a result of the increases in worker productivity due the industrial revolution of the late 1770s and 1800s. However, over the last 40 years, this long-term growth has stopped or slowed down."

The rate of return on capital investment now exceeds the rate of economic growth, part of the phenomenon known as financialization of the economy. Economist Thomas Picketty explains the result: a staggering increase in socioeconomic inequality. Within the developed economic world, a recent study by the Organisation for Cooperation and Economic Development estimates that the level of inequality in the developed world has been steadily rising for the last 50 years. On a global scale, the richest 300 people have more wealth than the poorest 3 billion, almost half the world's population. The extreme numbers give an idea of the scale of the deep social crisis through which we are now living. Any resolution of this crisis would involve a significant redistribution of economic resources, something that could be made permanent only on the basis of deep inroads into the prerogatives of private property under capitalism. It is hard to believe that the ruling class would be unaware of the ramifications. Bourgeois society has painted itself into a pretty tight corner.

The climate crisis is of similar significance. In a 2013 interview with the Boston Globe, Admiral Samuel Locklear, commander of United States forces in the Pacific, commented extensively on Asian affairs, singling out climate change as "probably the most likely thing that is going to happen . . . that will cripple the security environment, probably more likely than the other scenarios we all often talk about." He continued: "We have interjected into our multilateral dialogue—even with China and India—the imperative to kind of get military capabilities aligned [for] when the effects of climate change start to impact these massive populations," he said. "If it goes bad, you could have hundreds of thousands or millions of people displaced and then security will start to crumble pretty quickly."

The effects of climate change will not be limited to Asia. In the absence of an immigration policy commensurate with the climate crisis, Locklear's "imperative to kind of get military capabilities aligned" will consign to continued violence the millions who yearly make the effort to cross the U.S. border with Mexico. According to a report by the Congressional Research Service, "Border Patrol agent manpower assigned to the southwest border has been increasing steadily since the early 1990s. In 1992, there were 3,555 agents assigned to the southern border, by 2000 that number had increased by 141 percent to 8,580. Since 2000, the number of agents assigned to the southern border has continued to increase, more than doubling once more to 20,119 agents at the end of FY2009." This is more than at any time since President Wilson sent troops south to combat Pancho Villa, the Mexican revolutionary general. The number of Border Patrol agents as well as the incomprehensible number of deaths at the border, continue to increase.

Gramsci felt that capitalists would turn to coercive methods only if their effort to manufacture consent failed. Thus the turn to coercion may seem puzzling in light of the current lack of organization among forces opposed to capitalism. But in these days of pre-emptive strikes, it would be well to amend that view. Judging from Admiral Locklear's interview, the driving force may be pragmatic awareness within ruling circles of the need to hedge against social disorder: because there is no adequate effort to resolve them, the crises themselves are viewed as the competitors to bourgeois rule. The trend over the last 40 years to greater use of force is a phenomenon that is deeply embedded in the capitalist social order.

This analysis suggests that social resistance to state violence in the United States, both in the interior and at the border, will be of increasing significance to maintaining space for the people's democratic struggle. Angela Davis summed it up in a recent statement in Essence Magazine, "our work must be to continue taking to the streets and standing together against the routine actions of police and the DAs who collude with them; and continue saying, 'No Justice, No Peace, No Racist Police,' until there is real change on the agenda for us." Stepping up the campaign to debunk the racist ideology of criminality would be timely, and, on the theory that this is a teachable moment, it is also time to emphasize demands that point to the systemic nature of the problems, especially demands relating to the War on Drugs.

II. Policing on the Border.

The treacherous path to the north is first conceived among the poor, underprivileged, and exiled. Although the beauty and simple lifestyle of many Central and South American countries is worthy of the envy of the developed world, living among the corruption and violence of the governments and the criminal organizations is the daily bread many of us have to swallow, and digest. Meanwhile, the puny governments and their sicarios (hitmen) eat the mana produced by the hard-working and the oppressed.

Gustavo Alfredo Landaverde was the founder of the Christian Democratic Party (a conservative party in Honduras) and a congressman. In an interview with the Miami Herald in 2011, he said that the Honduran government is corrupted within its ranks by drug cartels and that he wanted to send a message to the organizations. They responded with their own message, three bullets for him, and one for his wife.

The War on Drugs, funded with large sums by the U.S. government, is one of the many sources of the social chaos that have made poor and rich Latin American countries seek new paths. For many, the governmental efforts to stop drug trafficking, are as reassuring as fucking for virginity. For others the path North in search of the "American dream" is as good an option as just waiting to be shot in the front of your house, in the middle of the day, to steal your old Nokia.

The major precursor to the mass movement and immigration of Latinos and indigenous people, is the violation of their sovereign economic choices and freedom to determine their own destiny. The repression and harassment of leftist movements since the Reagan era and the advent of the North American Free Trade Agreement in 1994, have made Central American countries the base of many studies in human rights violations. Dr. Ariadna Estevez from the National Autonomous University of Mexico, describes how human rights violations are associated with social conflicts, riots, and violent protest among other extreme events. To dissociate the causes from the effects would be not just a contradiction, but also historically and ethically unforgivable. Human rights violations have repercussions affecting both sides of the border, describes Dr. Estevez, "first, how human rights violations in the areas of temporary detention, the criminalization of migration ... Have negative consequences not only for migrants as individual subjects but also for receiving societies."

Dr. Estevez continues, adding that the "unskilled" labor force in poor countries attracts investment from corporations, the local states give these corporations tax breaks (in my own experience living in Honduras, sometimes these corporations pay no taxes at all), and this creates big gaps of inequality in poor countries where farmers and small local factories cannot compete with the cheap labor promoted by international firms. This, along with drug wars, governmental corruption and many other burdens, create a lack of the basic necessities, and a sense of frustration and powerlessness among the proletariat of the undeveloped world.

La Bestia is a necessary evil for the poor migrant. The Beast is a network of cargo trains that moves along Mexico's spine, carrying hundreds of migrants across the land, enduring rain, sun, dust storms, robberies, sexual assaults, and in many cases, death. The few that make it to the end of the line have to endure the punishing heat of the desert, and if that goes well, a welcome with rifle barrels and sweaty handcuffs by the U.S. border police, who are more than ready to stop them and deprive them of human rights and their dignity. It is to this part of the trip that recent news reports have turned their attention. The many children that show up alone at the border is a measure of the lengths to which parents will go when nothing else works. For many, leaving your child at the border under the supervision of the border police is a better option than having your child at home. That is the reality.

Caleb Maupin, an activist and political analyst, describes the rise of the symptoms of fascism in this excerpt:

"The rhetoric of these 'anti-immigrant activists' is classical fascist rhetoric. It calls for "restoring America's greatness" by purging 'undesirable' elements. It preaches extreme hatred not just for immigrants, impoverished people, and others, but also for any forces that seek to build solidarity with the oppressed. The "Tea Party", the John Birch Society, the Ku Klux Klan, the "militia groups" now being formed in Border States, all hate labor unions, anti-racist activists, and all who call for social equality. In their hate filled rants, they often speak obsessively about what they consider to be their ultimate enemy: Communism."

It is largely impossible to bring perpetrators of border violence to justice, since the Border Patrol agents, who are U.S. nationals, effectively cannot be prosecuted by the affected parties, who are not U.S. citizens. This situation makes immigrants as important to the Border Patrol as cattle. John Burnett of NPR explains that

> ". . . the American Immigration Council, an immigrant advocacy group, released a report that compiled the results of 809 complaints of excessive force and physical abuse. In the cases that were resolved, 97 percent led to "no action." Counseling was the discipline in most of the others, says Guillermo Cantor, senior policy analyst with the council."

The question of how to deal politically with violence in the borderlands should be a topic of extreme importance for the common revolutionary in the U.S., since its source is mostly rooted in the emergence of neoliberalism, neocolonialism and Washington's constant harassment of defenseless nations. The problem with reaching an agreement with parties, such as the DEA, that have the "control" or means to reach a resolution is that they themselves are plagued with corruption. For example, the head of the DEA Michelle Leonhart resigned in a wave of reports about DEA agents participating in prostitute-filled "sex parties" paid for by the Colombian drug cartels in 2001 and 2005. News of such caliber can be interpreted in the same way news of the Honduran Congressional corruption is perceived: corruption breeds death and incarceration of the poor.

On a last note, deaths on the border are generally rising since the early 1990s. There was a decrease in deaths for the 2014 fiscal year, but the numbers are still above average for the period from 1998-2009. The reality of the problem is that the deaths reported in the border areas by the Border Patrol and the National Foundation for American Policy only count cases in which the bodies are found on the U.S. side of the border. Deaths of immigrants in the Mexican territories or along the route are not included in the study from 1998 to 2014. In this study, the number reported by the Border Patrol is 6,707 deaths. The many bodies that decompose or simply erode to the elements and are never found are not accounted for in this figure. The problem of mass killings and clandestine graves also needs to be brought to light, whatever the geographical location or country in which they are found.

The deaths of immigrants at the hands of border vigilantes is also a fact not to be taken lightly. Groups labeling themselves as the patriots or citizen defenders, have sprung up along the border in recent years. They are mostly ex-military or civilian volunteers that patrol the border armed with pistols, rifles, and handcuffs. These so-called militia or vigilante groups alert Border Patrol agents when migrants are spotted. This is a very dangerous combination. One of the members of the community told the Reuters news site, that their son walks in the backyard with a shotgun slung on his back. The child is very likely just following a model that is widely promoted. The Southern Poverty Law Center has listed many of these groups in their A list of nativist extremists, and the Anti-Defamation League has observed that many of these groups work along side neo-nazi and white supremacist groups.

The Tactics of Border Police

Organized hate and defamation of migrants does not stop there. The very organization that is charged with upholding the law, the Border Patrol, has been linked to multiple cases of violence towards migrants in camps, including sexual assaults. According to an Aljazeera Op-Ed piece, from 2010 to 2014, border agents have killed 28 people, and face charges that include extortion, drug trafficking, theft, assault and rape. According to the article, Border Police use different tactics to abuse their power. One of their tactics is to stand in front of cars in order to justify shooting without remorse, so that when confronted they could say that it was in self defense. The U.S. Customs and Border Protection Agency (CBP) is funded by the U.S. government. It employs 60,000 people, and its budget is 12.4 billion dollars. On top of such alarming numbers is the fact that at least one agent is arrested daily for misconduct. The misconduct is lightly punished, and in many cases the atrocities do not make it to the public as was the case in March 2014, when a CBP officer arrested, kidnapped and raped three Honduran women, and tried to murder two of the women. The case stayed out of the public notice for two days, not because news source failed to announce such a crime, but because the CBP commissioner, Mr. Kerlikowske, delayed the announcement over insider politics.

And as bodies float in the Rio Grande, bodies rot in the Sonora desert, and human skeletons litter the land, the U.S. Customs and Border Protection Agency finds it in their best interest to propagate a song called "La Bestia." The song elaborates in artistic prose the characteristics of the trip north and the beast that takes you on it. U.S. Customs is as lost in its own interests as a migrant in a directionless desert. They believe that a song can inculcate fear among the populations of Honduras and El Salvador. They seem to be ignorant of the fact that as the climate changes, despite walls in the desert, or an increase in police abuses, migrants will keep coming. The thought that a simple blues song will change that is as efficient as border policing itself seems to be. The issue seems to be caught in a sad and dangerous balance, but the meek continue to march north, and the neglected and abused carry in their feet and hands the power of the Latino people. There should be at least as much freedom for people to cross the border as there is for capital.

III. History of Resistance, a Case Study.

Where there is oppression, there will be resistance. Such is the case in North Carolina as well, in particular in Raleigh, the capital city, after a spate of police killings of African-American men beginning in 1980 and continuing through a 10-year period ending in 1991 when Ivan Ingram was shot down by the police on Carver Street near St. Augustine's College in Raleigh's East Side Black neighborhood.

The first of the three killings that occurred in the 10-year span spurred the formation of the Black Workers for Justice (BWfJ) chapter in Raleigh. The killing occurred in the projects on Jones Street in downtown Raleigh. It began with a domestic disturbance that escalated, resulting in a call to the police, the presence of a white police officer and the death of a Black man.

Unfortunately, the coalition that was formed around the killing was short-lived as the organizations that normally got involved in issues, such as the NAACP, the Raleigh-Wake Citizens' Association and the newly-formed chapter of BWfJ were weak when it came to influence outside of the East Side, and when interest peaked a few weeks after the killing, things began to turn back to normal. However, by then, a larger coalition had formed around the Black United Front, a nationalist, multi-class organization headquartered in Chicago which breathed new life into the sometimey local single-issue coalition that had arisen around each police killing.

Things came to a head in 1984 when a mentally challenged man went off his medicine in the Boylan Heights area just west of downtown Raleigh. He was shot down and killed by a white policeman, which enraged the Black community. This time, under the Black United Front's coalition efforts, a large group of between 300 and 400 citizens marched from the East Side, with people coming from Boylan Heights, Oberlin Park and the West End Boulevard projects as well as the projects in Raleigh's North Side. The crowd gathered near the Post Office and marched down Hargett Street to the police station and held a spirited rally in Nash Square directly across the street from the police station. The rally called for the immediate resignation of the police chief, Fred Heineman, a recent import from New York and the formation of a civilian review board to police the police. The latter demand was thought to be unwinnable and so was abandoned early by the majority of the coalition, which was composed mostly of non-politically-oriented bourgeois elements (business owners, etc.)

Unfortunately, the Black United Front fell apart over other issues and the more progressive elements eventually joined in with BWfJ. In the years between 1981 and 1991, BWfJ had joined in with the Concerned Citizens for Educational Equity, a group of largely middle class Blacks who had been energized by the pro-segregation, neighborhood school movement that had developed among the white population, which would cause a throwback to the days of separate schools. These people were open to other issues of a nationalist character and so, when the killing of Ivan Ingram occurred, a new coalition was ready to move into action.

When Ivan Ingram was gunned down in early 1991, the Black community, already energized by several acts of brutality against Black citizens, as well as the growing polarization of the races around the educational issue of school resegregation, had several years work with at least two groups, BWfJ and Concerned Citizens for Educational Equity working together. This time, forming a coalition was relatively easy.

The committee directed a weekly march from the Carver Street site of Ivan's murder by the police to the Martin Luther King statue that had been erected some years earlier on Rock Quarry Road and MLK Boulevard. The refusal of the police department and the DA to bring charges against those responsible for the killing furthered the anger of the Black community and the polarization of the races within the city of Raleigh. Each week for several months a march was held with BWfJ and the Raleigh Citizens' Association, which the new coalition was called. The marches then began to reduce in numbers to around one per month for the next three year period. The coalition eventually split up when some elements pulled out over a political campaign around a right-wing candidate, to whom they lent their support. This coalition lasted longer than any other in modern times. Heineman retired shortly thereafter to run for congress and won one term in the throes of the polarization of the white population around the struggle for neighborhood schools; i.e., resegregation.

Despite the fact that these cases happened between 25 and 30 years ago, there are some things that are pretty much the same. One is that the strength and longevity of the struggle depends on the length of time that the individual groups in the coalition have spent working together over single and/or multi-race issues. The support around the Ingram case was relatively weak where coalition experience between groups was lacking. In these days, there was very little white citizen support for the struggle of Black people against police violence outside of the student population. This is still largely the case. The response from white citizens here in the South to the police murders of Walter Scott in Charleston, South Carolina and John Ferrell in Mecklenburg County, North Carolina and the police killing of a Mexican in Arizona have been tepid to non-existent. Unions have said nothing, which is not surprising, given their number.

One thing that appears hopeful is the emergence of proletarian and low-income youth into the struggle against police violence, in many cases taking the leadership as was done in Ferguson, Missouri. The Black Lives Matter movement is made up of large numbers of these youth, until now marginalized or seemingly unconcerned about large number of Black (and Brown) men slain by police over the past 40 or 50 years in mostly Northern cities. This element has taken control of the leadership in the Northern cities. Only time will tell which way things will go.

Jim Grant, recently the recipient of the ACLU of NC's Frank Porter Graham Award, plans to work on voting rights, educational justice, and a variety of other grassroots tasks until we are all free. As one of the Charlotte 3 civil rights activists who were framed by the State of North Carolina, his case marked the first time Amnesty International officially recognized that the United Stated holds political prisoners.

Daniel Mejia, originally from Honduras, is an organizer with the North Carolina Environmental Justice Network, a member of the Waterkeeper Alliance, and a farmer and carpenter in Eastern NC.

Zach Robinson, a member of the CCDS National Executive Committee, is a mathematician at East Carolina University and a community and labor activist in Greenville, NC.

Part Two: Austerity

The Fusion Politics Response to 21st Century Imperialism: From Arab Spring to Moral Mondays

By Harry Targ

Introduction

The deepening 21st century crises of capitalism - from growing economic impoverishment to neo-fascism to literal destruction of planet earth - demand movements and visions of change unparalleled in quantities and qualities of response. Anti-capitalist responses to these crises range from helplessness to spontaneous activism. Often political reactions ignore the history and context of the crises and the movements that have come before that have planted the seeds of fundamental social change. This paper will survey movements of social change in the era of neoliberal globalization suggesting both the breadth of such movements and the historical context from which they came. The tasks for today still require an analysis of the nature of existing systems and responses, visions of desirable alternatives, and contextualized discussions of moving from here to there. "Moving Beyond Capitalism" requires such a grounding of the future in the past and the present.

21st Century Imperialism: Post-Cold War Perspectives on Global Political Economy

The collapse of the Soviet Union transformed world affairs, scholarly analyses of international relations, punditry, and rationales for imperial foreign policies. A new buzzword became part of political discourse to describe the international system: "globalization." Almost immediately a large literature was generated suggesting that the world had changed. Globalization was replacing the system of often hostile nation-states that had characterized the world since the sixteenth century.[1]

'Moral Monday' mobilization in North Carolina

While interpretations of globalization varied, the common conception of the term suggested that a process of relations was occurring in which interactions between nations, business and financial organizations, groups, and peoples had become so frequent and intense that they were creating one global society.[2] Major globalizing institutions included multinational corporations, especially the 200 largest global corporations with production, distribution, and decision-making facilities in many countries, and international financial institutions engaged in speculative activities all across the globe. At the cultural level a handful of media conglomerates produced a large percentage of the cultural products, images, artistic endeavors, and print and electronic information that the world consumed. Finally, international institutions such as the World Bank, the International Monetary Fund, and the newly created World Trade Organization brought international influence to bear on states that resisted the globalization process.

In conjunction with the collapse of socialism on the world stage, apologists for globalization celebrated it as transformative, leading to a new world order.[3] With increasing interaction, it was claimed, old inter-state conflicts would be reduced in part because the salience of states was declining. Also, globalization was bringing people together with shared economic endeavors, social values, and culture. The process of global integration would over time lead to the creation of truly global institutions and society. And, some commentators suggested that globalization was an inevitable byproduct of a technological revolution.

Another set of theorists, global dialecticians,[4] responded to the new theorizing by reminding people that globalization was not new. In fact, they argued, globalization was a characteristic feature of capitalism as a mode of production. Marx, in The Communist Manifesto, recognized that capitalists sought markets, cheap labor and natural resources all across the globe. Having reminded readers of the historic nature of the globalization process, the global dialecticians suggested that particular features of contemporary history made the globalization process more likely; the United States as the last remaining superpower and the transformation of communications via the internet for example. For the dialecticians, the process of globalization was new and old at the same time. It had its roots in the rise of capitalism out of feudalism and it was transformed by economic, political, military, and technological changes that had occurred over the last fifty years.

Importantly for global dialecticians, "globalization" did not just happen. As a process globalization was encouraged by interests and institutionalized in policies promoted by the largest capitalist countries in the world. These policies were known everywhere (but the United States) as "neoliberal" policies. The name came from the historical labeling of classical political economy approaches that described and defended market, capitalist economies.

'Classical Liberalism' and Adam Smith

The theoretical foundation of "classical liberalism" in the economic sphere was linked to the writings of Adam Smith. The emphasis in Smith's theoretical paradigm as adopted by contemporary policy makers was the market, a venue for the buying and selling of commodities. Through this mythical market place, societies experienced individual freedom and economic development. Out of the self-interested conduct of "rational actors," the entire economic system survived, grew, and provided for the needs of most participants.

Politically, "liberalism" referred to the market place of political discourse and advocacy among diverse groups, each advocating public policies that met their interests. Political liberalism had its roots in philosophers such as John Locke, U.S. constitutional writer James Madison, French commentator on the United States Alexis De Tocqueville, and modern political scientists such as Robert Dahl, Nelson Polsby, and Theodore Lowi. Markets maximized individual and group behavior in the economic sphere and interest groups in the political sphere. That kind of liberalism was not the "big government" liberalism that talk show hosts targeted for constant rebuke. For analysts worldwide "neo" referred to the contemporary variant of the classical theories of Smith, Locke, and their compatriots.

Neoliberalism as it is understood in world affairs today constitutes a set of economic policies that governments adopt (or are forced to adopt) that promote globalization. These policies call for radically reduced government involvement in the economy and increased reliance on the global market place. Neoliberal policies have been imposed on most countries by international institutions that serve the interests of capitalist states and global capitalist interests, especially financial institutions and multinational corporations. [5]

Neoliberal international institutions that have the political and economic leverage to impose neoliberal policies on most countries include the International Monetary Fund (IMF), the World Bank, the World Trade Organization (WTO), the G8 countries (the largest capitalist countries), regional international organizations and trade regimes, and private banks and corporations. Neoliberal policies are imposed by one or more of these institutions on vulnerable countries, essentially to promote global penetration of their economies; thus expanding globalization.

Of special relevance to the imposition of neoliberal globalization was the increased debt that nations began to incur in the 1970s. As oil prices spiked - due initially to Middle East crises - and banks accumulated huge quantities of profit from oil sales, bankers needed to put the surplus profits to use. Nations were encouraged and/or forced to accumulate dramatically increased debt. Countries began to import more oil than their exported goods earned. They had to borrow money to continue their development programs. They then found themselves at the door steps of international financial institutions and borrowing began. In exchange for receiving loans, debtor countries were required to radically transform their economic programs. They were obliged to adopt neoliberal economic policies that spurred the process of globalization.

Neoliberal economic policies (sometimes referred to as policies of "austerity") included the following.

First, indebted nations were obliged to develop domestic policies that promoted "economic stabilization," which meant cutting government spending. Countries must shift from economies based on state/market collaboration to market driven economies, whatever the short-term costs to those citizens who had depended on public services for basic safety nets.

Second, neoliberal policies required "economic restructuring." Two key elements of restructuring included the privatization of public institutions. Many countries ran public institutions that provided services to their citizens: from health delivery, transportation, food subsidies, to public ownership of key natural resources. International financiers demanded that recipients of debt privatize their public institutions. From the time that the President of Mexico declared his country's bankruptcy in 1982 until the 1990s, 800 of some 1,100 state-owned enterprises in that country were privatized. Privatization became a global elite mantra, spreading even to core capitalist countries. The other element of restructuring was deregulation, the demand that government efforts to regulate the way the private sector operated needed to be eliminated. Regulations, it was claimed, impaired the "magic of the marketplace."

Third, countries receiving loans from international institutions were required to shift their economies from producing goods and services for domestic consumption to the development of exports. Countries were obliged to shift from diversification, often advocated in the 1960s, to the concentration on the production of a handful of commodities for sale on the world market. The goal was to earn scarce foreign exchange to pay back bankers and to channel foreign earnings into investments at home.

In the process countries, such as Mexico, which produced products, food for its people for example shifted to produce small numbers of goods for which there was international demand. The Mexican economy which enjoyed food self-sufficiency, with large percentages of the food produced by small farmers on individual plots of land and in cooperatives, began to produce broccoli, flowers, strawberries and other crops for sale in United States markets. The land was transformed into "factories in the fields" owned by huge agricultural corporations, while Mexico was forced to import corn for tortillas. From the 1970s to the present the neoliberal economic programs increased global penetration of local economies and reduced the capacity of these local economies to remain sovereign and self-sustaining.

Analysts of neoliberal globalization disagreed on its impacts. Globalization celebrants argued that the neoliberal policies in conjunction with the new technology would transform the world from underdevelopment to development and from domestic and international strife to harmony.

Transfer of Jobs

Critics of neoliberal globalization, largely the followers of theories of imperialism and dependency saw growing gaps between the rich and poor, between countries and within countries directly attributable to the new policies. They saw a vast transfer of jobs from the industrial capitalist countries to poor countries where wages were lower and worker rights weaker. Dictatorial and class-divided societies facilitated foreign capital penetration at the expense of peripheral peoples. The economic divisions were exacerbated by cataclysmic environmental changes. And, since the end of the Cold War the frequency and magnitude of violence and war increased rather than decreased.

As to foreign policy, the "last remaining superpower," as the United States was conceptualized, articulated a pro-active approach to world affairs rather than an "anti-communist" approach; that is the promotion of "market democracies."

The State in the Era of Neoliberal Globalization

Among the critics of neoliberal globalization a significant debate emerged. Some writers argued that the state system still anchored, induced, and maintained neoliberal globalization. The United States remained the last remaining superpower but it worked in alliance with the other leading capitalist powers. Leaders of the G7 countries (the United States, Great Britain, Canada, France, Italy, Germany, and Japan) met annually to deliberate on the state of the world. After the fall of Soviet socialism, Russia was admitted to the select circle.

The United States took the lead economically, politically, and militarily in guiding global society in partnership with the other seven. In addition, each country pursued its own individual interests as well and all maintained alliances with smaller and weaker regimes. The first Gulf War, for example, was carried out under US direction but with the support of some thirty countries, big and small.

Some theorists argued, from their understanding of the continued application of military force and the power the G7 held over international economic institutions that states still mattered. It was the state that maintained the force and regulated economic activities in world affairs. Ruling class control of the instrumentalities of the state still determined how successful global capitalism would be in the twenty-first century. S

New Transnational Capitalist Class

Other theorists suggested that globalization and the concentration of economic power was creating a transnational ruling class that dominated the economic and political life of the global political economy.[6] They pointed to the transnational character of corporations, with their manufacturing facilities everywhere and headquarters in a variety of countries. Financial speculation, which defined the twenty-first century international system, occurred instantaneously all across the globe. The last barriers to transnational class rule came down with so-called "free trade" agreements such as the North America Free Trade Agreement (NAFTA) and the new world trade regime, the World Trade Organization (WTO). The exercise of state and local sovereignty became a violation of international agreements.

The transnational ruling class included the biggest, most powerful capitalists in the world who worked in conjunction with junior partners in weaker countries. Years ago, peace researcher Helge Hveem referred to an incipient "global dominance system" that was stratified from the apex of wealth and power to the very poor and oppressed. Those at the base of the diamond- shaped global society may have the power to make local decisions but lack the capacity to affect the global political economy. That capacity resides, he said, at the top. In this schema, the salience of nation-states was dramatically reduced. The transnational ruling class ruled.

While CEOs of corporations and banks, chairs of international organizations, presidents of the most prestigious universities, and an occasional trade union leader continued to have enormous latitude to direct international policy in the new century, they continued to rely on the instrumentalities of the state to maintain stability in the face of growing opposition. The new century was fraught with war and high and low tech military interventions. And increasingly as economic crisis imposed itself on the global economy, ruling classes in various countries disagreed on the direction of future policy. And finally, with the rise of resistance from the Global South and within countries from rebellious workers, youth, and indigenous peoples, the state assumed renewed importance as an instrumentality of repression. The state, it seemed, was almost as relevant in the era of neoliberal globalization as before.

The Transformation of the Relations of Production

The transformation from Socialist or heterodox policies in the Global South to neo-liberalism, while not stimulating incorporation into the global economy and development as promised, did facilitate changing work patterns. Neo-liberal policies, including privatization and shifting production from domestic consumption to exports, radically transformed rural work in many countries of the Global South.

Governmental pressures undermined traditional patterns of agriculture including land ownership and production processes. Land holdings were consolidated under the control of foreign or wealthy domestic investors. More productive and larger agricultural units began to produce commodities for sale in rich overseas markets. Peasant farmers who in the past produced food stuffs for domestic consumption were replaced by agricultural workers and new technologies to produce winter vegetables and flowers for foreign customers. Countries which had produced enough food for their own people became net importers of food products. In addition, agricultural subsidies characteristic of the United States and countries of the European Union made it all but impossible for poor farmers to compete with the cheap imported food.

As a result of the new agriculture, and farmers forced off their land, migration to urban centers magnified, as more and more rural dwellers sought work. Cities in the Global South doubled or tripled in size, becoming surrounded by make-shift dwellings of people looking for work. Some rural migrants were able to find work in the new export-processing zones or sweat shop industries rising in some countries of the Global South. The pool of cheap labor in the Global South, replenished by the transformation of agriculture, provided an attractive opportunity for textile, electronics, and other manufacturing employment, once basic to the manufacturing economies of the industrialized countries. The globalization of production occurred in tandem with the imposition of neo-liberal economic policies, and the transformation of agriculture.

These changes were reflected in changing employment/unemployment rates and the kind of work that became available in the Global South. From 1950 to 1990, there was a decline by almost 1/3 of those of working age in the world engaged in agriculture. The percentage of the world work force in agriculture in 1990 was down to 49%, from 67% in 1950 (In Latin America and the Caribbean the decline from 1950 to 1990 was from 54% to 25% in agriculture).

In addition, the growth in industrial employment between 1950 and 1990 was modest, not commensurate with the declining agricultural employment. (In Latin America, the decline in agriculture was more dramatic than the world figures while the increase in industrial employment was not greater than the world figures). International Labor Organization (ILO) data suggested that in the world at large "the share of employment in manufacturing declined between 1990 and 2001 in all economies for which data are available..."(ILO, 21 Nov. 2005).

Further, the world data (and the data for Latin America) indicated that the major sectoral growth in employment has been in the service sector. Increases in service sector employment ranged from 8% to 16% among countries in different economic strata. The largest growth in the service sector occurred in the lower-middle income countries.

Finally, the most significant shift in employment throughout the world, particularly in the Global South, has been from the formal economy (agriculture, industry, and service) to the informal economy. Most workers in this growing sector of the work force are driven by a desperate need to provide the rudiments of life. Consequently, they are willing to do virtually anything to earn money. This may involve lucrative small street market sales, or low wage home work (from house cleaning to garment assembly), or prostitution, or drug dealing. Work in the informal economy is not regulated. Workers enjoy no work place health and safety protections. They receive no health or retirement benefits. And, of negative consequence to the national government, they pay no taxes.

In a report produced by the Department of Economic and Social Affairs of the United Nations, "The Inequality Predicament,"[7] a distinction was made between "haves" and "have-nots" in terms of employment. The former are employed in the formal economy. They are more likely "... to earn decent wages, receive job-related benefits, have secure employment contracts and be covered by relevant laws and regulations" (UN, 2005, 29). The informal sector represented the polar opposite in terms of wages, benefits, rights, and expectations of the regularity of work. The growth of the informal sector worldwide, the report said, was intimately tied to growing global inequality.

The UN report estimated that "informal employment accounts for between one half and three quarters of non-agricultural employment in the majority of developing countries." They indicated that the percentage of those who worked in the informal sector varied across the Global South: 48% in North Africa, 51% in Latin America and the Caribbean, 65 % in Asia and 78% in Sub-Saharan Africa (UN, 30).

In addition, the report referred to studies that suggested that the informal sector accounted for significant shares of the overall income and gross domestic product of individual countries. One study of 110 countries in 2000 found that the 18% of the gross national incomes of OECD countries came from the informal sector, 38% in "transition" countries (formerly Socialist), and 41% in developing countries. The informal economy accounted for 42% of the GNP in Africa, 26% in Asia, and 41% in Latin America (UN, 30-34).

The New Precarious Classes: the Precariat

Data shows that unemployment around the world rose over the period from 1993 to 2002 and declined somewhat in 2003. What may be the most significant finding from this data is the fact that the seeming recovery of 2003 only imperceptibly impacted on unemployment rates. Even if sectors of the global economy experienced growth, some theorists suggested, recovery given the system of global capitalism was "jobless." As recently as 2014 the International Labor Organization reported that on a global basis "the number of unemployed and discouraged workers continues to increase."[8]

The economic transformations initiated in the Global South in the 1970s occurred in the context of the concentration and globalization of capital and the declining resistance including the collapse of Socialism. The oil crisis, the rise of a global debt system, global policy shifts from state/market economies to neo-liberalism paralleled significant changes in work activity from agriculture and industry to service, to the rise of the informal sector and unemployment. The end product of these transformations has been increasing global inequality in wealth and income and the continuation of massive poverty, powerlessness, and precariousness.
While rates of poverty declined over the last twenty years of the twenti-

eth century still half the world's population in 2001 lived on less than $2 a day. And the percentage declines in extreme poverty, less than $1 a day, during this period masked the fact that more people in 2001 were in extreme poverty than twenty years earlier. The numbers of people in extreme poverty increased in Latin America and the Caribbean, the Middle East and North Africa, South Asia, Sub-Saharan Africa, and India. The numbers of those in poverty declined in East Asia and the Pacific and China.

Also, it is clear that income inequality has been increasing between richer and poorer regions of the globe. With the OECD countries representing the rich countries, on a per capita income basis, shares of income of peoples in Sub-Saharan Africa, South Asia, the Middle East and North Africa, Latin America and the Caribbean have declined between 1980 and 2001. Weller, Scott, and Hersch (2001) reported that in 1980 median income in the richest countries (top ten percent) was 77 times greater than the median income in the poorest countries (the bottom ten percent). By 1999, the gap had expanded to 122 times. In 2005, the wealthiest 20 percent of the world's population accounted for 76.6 percent of the world's private consumption. As recently as 2013, 3 billion people lived on less than $2.50 a day.

The transformation of employment from agriculture and industry to service and the informal sector-a shift that has been characterized as one from "have" to "have-not" jobs-has been reflected in the continuation of massive poverty around the globe and substantial evidence that the distribution of wealth and income has worsened over the period of neo liberal policy influence. "The Inequality Predicament" made it clear as well that income inequality was reproduced in the distribution of access to health care, education, housing, access to water, and sanitation.

As suggested above, data like these led Samir Amin (2003) to predict that the transformation of the global political economy was precipitating a crisis of poverty and human misery that will transcend the expectations of the most well-meaning humanists. Amin described the emergence of "precarious classes" in both rural and urban areas. Estimating that half the world's population (3 billion people) lived in the country, he predicted that nearly 2.8 billion of them would become economically redundant. That is, given technology, 20 million people could provide the food needs for the planet. In the cities, 1.5 billion of 3 billion people were marginalized workers who experienced work temporarily and/or who always lived with the insecurity of job and income loss. Over four billion people of the six billion living on the planet, Amin wrote, constituted "the precarious classes," made redundant because of declining employment and being reduced to perpetual employment insecurity due to the exigencies of the pursuit of profit in an era of neo-liberal globalization. This situation, Amin asserted, constituted a coming global crisis not seen in human history. And this was before the global economic crisis that began in 2007 which was followed by global protest against dramatically escalating economic insecurity, authoritarian regimes, and outrage at a continually growing economic inequality and political powerlessness.

In a recent book, Guy Standing,[9] former Director of the International Labor Organization Socio-Economic Security Program, echoed Amin's characterization of a decade ago. "The precariat consists of a growing number of people around the world who live in social and economic insecurity, without occupational identities, drifting in and out of jobs and constantly worried about their incomes, housing and much else.[10] He coined the term by combining "precarious" and "proletariat." He warned that: "Unless the cries from the precariat are heard, the stirrings that have been heard and seen in the streets and squares of Greece, Spain, England and elsewhere will only be the harbinger of much more anger and upheaval."

Resistance From Below

Vijay Prashad published an interesting volume in 2007, T*he Darker Nations: A People's History of the Third World*, that appropriately made the narrative of world history more complicated. As the sub-title suggested, Prashad was inspired to reexamine post-World War II international history from the lens of Howard Zinn's classic history, A People's History of the United States. The fundamental proposition of the Zinn volume was that history is not just made by the powerful (monarchs, generals, popes, bankers, CEOs of major corporations or even hegemonic states) but by masses of people who have lacked the traditional attributes of power. Zinn's history of the United States emphasized the role of native peoples, workers, women, people of color, and peace and justice activists in shaping the larger political and economic agendas of the United States. Zinn's approach, along with a new literature on labor studies, African-American studies, and Women's Studies, suggested that historical change was the resultant of the dialectical, often conflicted, struggles between the rich and powerful and the weak and powerless.

Prashad applied the Zinn methodology to the history of international relations in the twentieth century. The Darker Nations describes the rise of anti-colonial struggles, the emergence of newly independent nation-states out of global colonial empires, the creation of solidarity among elites from these "new" nations, and the efforts they engaged in to gain influence over global economics and politics to make the international system work for them.
Prashad described the creation of the non-aligned movement; a body of

nations prioritizing global economic justice rather than attachment to one or another Cold War superpower. He discussed international conferences that addressed the exploitative character of the global economy, brutal and desperate wars to maintain colonialism, the condition of women, and overcoming the bipolar world. Attention was given to the Global South's introduction of the idea of a New International Economic Order (NIEO) which included proposals for reforming the global economy. Prashad pointed out that for a time, with US/Soviet contestation for the "hearts and minds" of the new nations, the NIEO figured prominently in debate in international organizations.

Prashad's story is also a story of the declining power of the countries of the Global South, as the first generation of anti-colonial leaders left the scene, some countries embraced neoliberal policies, and political factionalism grew in many countries. But, Prashad suggests, world affairs must be seen as a resultant of the dialectical relations between the core and periphery, a view not too different from that proposed by dependency theorists.

However, Prashad's story departs from Zinn's in that Prashad concentrates on states and elites in the Global South, and social/political movements less so. A real 'bottom-up" portrait of global struggle would include a much expanded portrait of grassroots movements for social change, sometimes involving cross-national networks of relationships. An updated rendition of the Prashad portrait of world affairs would have to include the global impacts of Arab spring, the uprisings in the Heartland of the United States, the Occupy movement in the United States, the more recent Moral Mondays campaign, and its reverberations all across the Global North and South. Theory about twenty-first century global life should draw upon theories of imperialism and dependency, bringing challenges from the Global South to the history, and elements of theories of globalization and neoliberalism that suggest cross-national connections of peoples' movements from the grassroots, often motivated by protests against the neoliberal policy agenda.

Global Mobilizations and the History of Resistance

Just as globalization today has its roots in five hundred years of trade, investment, exploitation, and capital accumulation, the global justice movements of our day also have their roots in the patterns of resistance since the beginning of capitalism.

In a recent article Zahara Heckscher[11] pointed out that: "In virtually every society the Europeans invaded, people rose up to protest the cruelty of slavery, theft of land, and plunder of resources." While many of the protests were local, provoked by singular transgressions, and were inwardly oriented (from destroying crops to committing suicide to fleeing), many were national in their mobilization or even international.

Heckscher provided examples of resistance movements against globalization that occurred well before "the Battle of Seattle" in 1999. For example, the Tupac Amaru II uprising in Peru (1780-1781) was a multi-class, multi-ethnic rebellion of 6,000 armed protestors who opposed the effort of the Spanish colonial government to impose tariff reductions to flood local markets with cheap Spanish goods, increase taxes, and in other ways force economic integration between the colony and the Spanish economy.

Heckscher also offered the example of nineteenth century cross-national campaigns to ban slavery. She described the social movements in Europe that vigorously opposed the brutal Belgium colonial administration of the Congo at the end of the nineteenth century. She reflected on the efforts of the First International Workingmen's Association in Geneva to prohibit manufacturers from importing strikebreakers to replace striking workers. In the process, workers from Europe and North America began to mobilize in solidarity against an increasingly cross-national capitalism. Finally, in her brief survey she mentioned the Anti-Imperialist Movement that opposed U.S. occupation and control of the Philippines after 1898.

Each of these movements addressed economic and political issues together. Each was a response to the globalization of a great power, usually in pursuit of economic exploitation. And each of these movements created a shared consciousness, a solidarity among resisters across national boundaries. Even these movements were responses to local issues they represented a form of resistance to the globalization of capitalism.

The World Social Forum

At the dawn of the new century, a new tradition, inspired by the hundreds of years of resistance, was launched. Ten thousand activists-representing 1,000 groups from 120 countries, industrial and agricultural workers, indigenous peoples, environmentalists, anti-globalization activists -met at the World Social Forum in Porto Alegre, Brazil in January, 2001. This disparate assembly shared one idea: "Another World is Possible."

Naomi Klein[12] reported on this first WSF highlighting its exuberant and chaotic character. Neither defining it as a strength or a weakness she pointed out the fact that "...what seemed to be emerging organically out of the World Social Forum (despite the best efforts of some of the organizers) was not a movement for a single global government but a vision for an increasingly connected international network of very local initiatives, each built on direct democracy."

Subsequent to the first WSF, the organizing committee prepared a "Charter of Principles" which included the following: providing an environment for open and democratic debate; becoming a permanent process of building alternatives, particularly building a "world process;" bringing together and linking civil society groups, NGOs, and social movements from all countries; and increasing "the capacity for non-violent social resistance to the process of dehumanization" and introducing "onto the global agenda the change-inducing practices" that could create a "new world in solidarity."

The US Social Forum

Each year after, the WSF met in Brazil or India, or Kenya, or Venezuela. In 2007, a U.S. Social Forum was held in Atlanta, Georgia. Ten thousand people, mostly young and people of color attended the hundreds of panels and plenary sessions. Over 100 local and national groups displayed their literature and dialogued with conference participants.

As their call suggested: "The US Social Forum is more than a conference, more than a networking bonanza, more than a reaction to war and repression. The USSF will provide space to build relationships, learn from each other's experiences, share our analysis of the problems our communities face, and bring renewed insight and inspiration."[13]

Activists from nearly 100 organizations held the next US Social Forum which took place June 22-26, 2010 in Detroit. It occurred in the midst of a global economic crisis, multiple wars, the rise of neo-fascist forces around the world, and efforts of the United States to forestall the rising global resistance to neo-liberalism.

The National Planning Committee indicated that the USSF would address movement building, organizing and outreach, and improving structure and programming of the USSF movement. Of particular relevance to 2010, they wrote, were the following goals:[14]

" Strengthen and expand progressive infrastructure for long-term collaboration and work for fundamental change.
" Disseminate effective models for democratic participation and movement building.
" Shape and influence the public conversation in ways that convey momentum and hope.
" Model diverse, representative movement building that is cross-cutting, democratic, and effectively integrates process and outcomes.

" Continue to be a space in which grassroots lead, while being inclusive of other sectors. Develop a collective systemic understanding and analysis of the current economic and political moment.
" Create a shared vision of the society and world that challenges poverty and exploitation, all forms of oppression, militarism and war, and environmental destruction.
" Articulate and practice concrete internationalism through consciousness of today's global context and the power of radical movements in the Global South, and awareness of our power in coming from the US and our responsibility to the broader international movement.
" Identify convergences that have already happened.
" Work toward greater convergence between working class struggles and progressive movements.
" Build on the strengths and convergences of the 2007 USSF.
" Further develop Black, Immigrant and Indigenous Nations' solidarity.

The goals and vision of the US Social Forum were truly ambitious. It was unclear how the Social Forum movement could create enough ideological commonality, organizational structure, leadership sensitive to its grassroots base, and global solidarity to make another world possible. It was clear however that the Social Forum movement was part of a long history of resistance and struggle against capitalism, and as such is as necessary now as at any time in history.

World Protests 2006-2013[15]

Isabel Ortiz, Sara Burke, Mohamed Berrada, and Hernan Cortes, Institute for Policy Dialogue and Freidrich-Ebert-Stiftung New York,[16] reported on a longitudinal project of 843 protest incidents between 2006 and 2013 in 87 countries, categorizing these incidents by grievances, participants, protest methods, targets of protest, achievements, forms of repression, and the major policy demands of protestors. They found an increase in protest events every year with a particular spike in such activities after the onset of the 2010 financial crisis and the concomitant austerity measures that most governments adopted to stem the crisis at the expense of the vast majorities of people. About a third of protests occurred in higher income countries, and twenty percent in Latin American and Caribbean countries but protest activity seemed to emerge all across the globe.

More than half the protests related to economic justice and anti-austerity issues and a little less than half were about lack of democracy. Often multiple issues motivated protests and these included global justice and human rights issues. The authors claimed that twenty-five percent of the protests linked the lack of economic justice to a parallel lack of democracy. The data indicated that protesters included traditional activists, trade unionists, and an array of young and older protestors "...who are increasingly joining activists from all kinds of movements, not only in marches and rallies...but in a new framework of protest that includes civil disobedience and direct action..." They list as newer forms of protest computer hackers and whistleblowers. Data showed that violence and looting occurred in less than ten percent of the cases.

The data indicates that protests are allayed against governments and policy-makers but also target corporations, political and economic elites, the financial sector, and dominant global economic institutions such as the IMF and the World Bank. While protestors usually did not achieve their goals, data indicated that the size of protest activities had increased and some have led to longer term organizing efforts. The authors concluded from their research: "The set of policies at the national and global levels to address the grievances ...cross over virtually every area of public policy, from jobs, public services, and social protection to taxation, debt, and trade." Basic to all the protests is "the demand of real democracy."

The Project of the Darker Nations Today

What we have witnessed over the last two years perhaps constitutes what Prashad, regards as a new stage in the development of the Third World Project.

First, the Middle East revolution, if we wish to call it that for shorthand reasons, can be seen as a direct reaction to the profound global economic crisis that has been brought on by neoliberal globalization.

Second, it clearly is motivated by goals similar to those the Non-Aligned Movement (NAM) endorsed in the 1950s, that is some kind of New International Economic Order.

Third, the movements seem to be secular, as well as religious, perhaps reflecting a rejection of the counterrevolutionary programs of Third World elites who promoted division and reaction to further their own interests.

Fourth, the movements appear to incorporate vast numbers of young people, men and women, workers and small business people, intellectuals and artists, as well as those who identify with their religious traditions.

Fifth, the labor movement and the growing percentages of unemployed and underemployed workers have been playing a passionate and committed role in the struggles. The estimated 40 percent of the world's population in the so-called "informal sector" have a stake in revolutionary change as do workers in transportation, electronics, construction, and manufacturing.

Sixth, this revolution has been largely a nonviolent revolution. "Revolutionaries" are saying no or enough, and are doing so in such numbers that the institutions of government and the economy cannot continue to operate. This culls up memories of the Gandhi struggles against the British empire and the civil rights movement in the U.S. South.

Seventh, this is an electronic revolution. As a result of the computer age, time and space as factors confounding communicating and organizing have been eliminated. Cell phones and social networks do not make revolutions but they facilitate the kind of organizing that historically was more tedious and problematic.

And, the new technology insures that revolutionary ferment in one part of the world can be connected to revolutionary ferment elsewhere. In a certain sense, now all youth can be participants, not just observers.

In a recent interview Prashad summarized some of these elements of the ongoing struggles:

"The Arab revolt that we now witness is something akin to a "1968" for the Arab World. Sixty per cent of the Arab population is under 30 (70 per cent in Egypt). Their slogans are about dignity and employment. The resource curse brought wealth to a small population of their societies, but little economic development. Social development came to some parts of the Arab world...

The educated lower-middle-class and middle-class youth have not been able to find jobs. The concatenations of humiliations revolts these young people: no job, no respect from an authoritarian state, and then to top it off the general malaise of being a second-class citizen on the world stage...was overwhelming. The chants on the streets are about this combination of dignity, justice, and jobs" [17]

Some of the Differences From Before

Comparing the period of the Third World Project with today suggests some differences and similarities. As Prashad and other historians of the Third World make clear, the rise of the non-aligned movement gained some influence because of the Cold War contest between the Soviet Union and the United States.

Now the world consists of a variety of new powers, some from the original movement (such as India, China, Egypt, and Brazil) whose economic, political, and military capabilities are challenging the traditional power structures of international relations. Also, global capitalism is in profound crisis and the causes of the revolutionary ferment as well as its escalation are intimately connected with the Middle East revolutions.

Today the danger of escalating state violence and repression remains significant. Global capitalism is in crisis. Some Third World regimes are still driven by fundamentalisms of one sort or another. And, finally, key decision makers in centers of global power seem committed still to archaic ideologies, for example suggesting that Islamic fundamentalism will take over revolutions, democracy is dangerous, and that the one "democracy" in the Middle East, Israel, will be further threatened by the movements in the region.

In addition, the Egyptian revolution, while exciting and inspirational, suffered from some of the same weaknesses Prashad described at the dawn of the Third World Project. Looking back 50 years, the leaders, and the various participating sectors of the mass movement, had not articulated a systematic and compelling ideology, beyond the programmatic demands of the NIEO.

Several countries in the forefront of the NAM were military regimes. Placards of Nasser were prominently displayed in Liberation Square during Arab spring. Nasser was a military leader of the "Free Colonels" movement that overthrew King Farouk in 1952. The same "revolutionary" military created a Hasni Mubarak many years later. While the military in Egypt today may act in ways that curry the favor of the protesters, it must be clear that military institutions are driven by their own interests, not the interests of the people.

So the mass mobilizations since early 2011 that were so exciting, inspiring hope for the world, have been fraught with danger. The people now must struggle to articulate, advocate for, and institutionalize a program of humane socialism in every country where they are victorious. The task of progressives in the Global North is to support the new project and to link its causes and visions to the struggles that are experienced everywhere.

Protest Movements in the United States

Along with anecdotal evidence, aggregate data confirms the continuation and expansion of activist groups and protest activities all across the face of the globe. For example in the United States, Mark Solomon in an important essay "Whither the Socialist Left? Thinking the 'Unthinkable'" discusses the long history of socialism in the United States, the brutal repression against it, damaging sectarian battles on the left, the miniscule size of socialist organizations today and yet paradoxically the growing sympathy for the idea of socialism among Americans, particularly young people. He calls for "the convergence of socialist organizations committed to non-sectarian democratic struggle, engagement with mass movements, and open debate in search of effective responses to present crises and to projecting a socialist future." Again, the Solomon article does not conceptualize "left unity" and "building the progressive majority" as separate and distinct projects but as fundamentally interconnected. For him, and many others, the role of the left in the labor movement and other mass movements gave shape, direction, and theoretical cohesion to the battles that won worker rights in the 1930s.

Solomon's call has stimulated debate among activists around the idea of "left unity." The appeal for left unity is made more powerful by socialism's appeal, the current global crises of capitalism, rising mobilizations around the world, and living experiments with small-scale socialism such as the construction of a variety of workers' cooperatives.

Effective campaigns around "left unity" in recent years have prioritized "revolutionary education," drawing upon the tools of the internet to construct an accessible body of theory and debate about strategy and tactics that could solidify left forces and move the progressive majority into a socialist direction. The emerging Online University of the Left (OUL), an electronic source for classical and modern theoretical literature about Marxism, contemporary debates about strategy and tactics, videos, reading lists, and course syllabi, constitute one example of left unity. The OUL serves as resource for study groups, formal coursework, and discussions among socialists and progressives. Those who advocate for "left unity" or left "convergence" celebrate these many developments, from workers cooperatives to popular education, as they advocate for the construction of a unified socialist left.

The Occupy Movement, first surfacing in the media in September, 2011, initiated and renewed traditions of organized and spontaneous mass movements around issues that affect peoples' immediate lives such as housing foreclosure, debt, jobs, wages, the environment, and the negative role of money in US politics. Perhaps the four most significant contributions of the Occupy Movement include:

1. Introducing grassroots processes of decision-making.
2. Conceptualizing modern battles for social and economic justice as between the one percent (the holders of most wealth and power in society) versus the 99 percent (weak, economically marginalized, and dispossessed, including the precariat).
3. Insisting that struggles for radical change be spontaneous, often es-

chewing traditional political processes.
4. Linking struggles locally, nationally, and globally.

During the height of Occupy's visibility some 500 cities and towns experienced mobilizations around social justice issues. While significantly less today, Occupy campaigns still exist, particularly in cities where larger progressive communities reside. Calls for left unity correctly ground their claims in a long and rich history of organized struggle while "occupiers" and other activists today have been inspired by the bottom-up and spontaneous uprisings of 2011 (both international and within the United States).

Building a Progressive Majority

A third, and not opposed, approach to political change at this time has been labeled "building a progressive majority." This approach assumes that large segments of the U.S. population agree on a variety of issues. Some are activists in electoral politics, others in trade unions, and more in single issue groups. In addition, many who share common views of worker rights, the environment, health care, undue influence of money in politics, immigrant rights etc. are not active politically. The progressive majority perspective argues that the project for the short-term is to mobilize the millions of people who share common views on the need for significant if not fundamental change in economics and politics.

Often organizers conceptualize the progressive majority as the broad mass of people who share views on politics and economics that are "centrist" or "left." Consequently, over the long run, "left" participants see their task as three-fold. First, they must work on the issues that concern majorities of those at the local and national level. Second, they struggle to convince their political associates that the problems most people face have common causes (particularly capitalism). Third, "left" participants see the need to link issues so that class, race, gender, and the environment, for example, are understood as part of the common problem that people face.

At this point in time as the recent data set called "Start" shows (http://www.startguide.org/orgs/orgs00.html) there are some "500 leading organizations in the United States working for progressive change on a national level." START divided these 500 organizations into twelve categories based on their main activities. These include progressive electoral, peace and foreign policy, economic justice, civil liberties, health advocacy, labor, women's and environmental organizations. Of course their membership, geographic presence, financial resources, and strategic and tactical vision vary widely. And, many of the variety of progressive organizations at the national level are reproduced at the local and state levels as well.

In sum, when looking at social change in the United States at least three emphases are being articulated: left unity, the Occupy, and building a progressive majority. Each highlights its own priorities as to vision, strategy, tactics, and political contexts. In addition, the relative appeal of each may be affected by age, class, gender, race, and issue prioritization as well. However, these approaches need not be seen as contradictory. Rather the activism borne of each approach may parallel the others.

The Emergence of Moral Mondays in the US South

Moral Mondays refers to a burgeoning mass movement that had its roots in efforts to defend voter rights in North Carolina. Thousands of activists have been mobilizing across the South over the last year inspired by Moral Mondays. They are fighting back against draconian efforts to destroy the right of people to vote, workers' and women's rights, and for progressive policies in general. Paradoxically, many progressives in the South and elsewhere have not heard of this budding movement.

Moral Mondays began as the annual Historic Thousands on Jones Street People's Assembly (HKonJ) in 2006 to promote progressive politics in North Carolina. Originally a coalition of 16 organizations, initiated by the state's NAACP, it has grown to include 150 organizations today promoting a multi-issue agenda. In 2006, its task was to pressure the state's Democratic politicians to expand voting rights and support progressive legislation on a variety of fronts.

With the election of a tea-party government in that state in 2012, the thrust of Moral Mondays shifted to challenging the draconian policies threatening to turn back gains made by people of color, workers, women, environmentalists and others. Public protests at the state house weekly in the spring of 2013 during the state legislative session led to over 1,000 arrests for civil disobedience and hundreds of thousands of hits on MM websites. Similar movements have spread throughout the South (Georgia, South Carolina, and Florida) and in some states in the Midwest and Southwest (Wisconsin, Pennsylvania, and Missouri).

To kick off the spring 2014 protests, MM organizers called a rally in Raleigh, North Carolina on February 8 which brought out at least 80,000 protestors. Rev. William Barber, a key organizer of the movement, has grounded this new movement in history, suggesting that the South is in the midst of the "third reconstruction." The first reconstruction, after the Civil War, consisted of Black and white workers struggling to create a democratic South (which would have impacted on the North as well). They elected legislators who wrote new state constitutions to create democratic institutions in that region for the first time. This first reconstruction was destroyed by white racism and the establishment of Jim Crow segregation.

The second reconstruction occurred between Brown vs. Board of Education in 1954 and President Nixon's 1968 "Southern Strategy." During this period formal segregation was overturned, Medicare and Medicaid were established, and Social Security was expanded. Blacks and whites benefited. Dr. King's 1968 Poor People's Campaign envisioned a defense and expansion of the second reconstruction.

Now we are in the midst of a third reconstruction, according to Barber. Political mobilizations today, like those of the first reconstruction, are based on what was called in the 1860s "fusion" politics; that is bringing all activists-Black, Brown, white, gay/straight, workers, environmentalists-together. Fusion politics assumes that only a mass movement built on everyone's issues can challenge the billionaire economic elites such as the Koch brothers and their Wall Street collaborators with masses of people (the 99 percent). Fusion politics, he says, requires an understanding of the fact that every issue is interconnected causally with every other issue. Therefore, democracy, civil rights, labor, women's, gay/lesbian, and environmental movements must act together (http://youtu.be/sOMn8jLjVLE).

At the February action in Raleigh five general demands were articulated as guides for their spring activism. While economic, political, and historical forces vary from state to state the demands can serve as a model for action elsewhere as well. The North Carolina demands are:

"   Secure pro-labor, anti-poverty policies that insure economic sustainability;
"   Provide well-funded, quality public education for all;
"   Stand up for the health of every North Carolinian by promoting health care access and environmental justice across all the state's communities;
"   Address the continuing inequalities in the criminal justice system and ensure equality under the law for every person, regardless of race, class, creed, documentation or sexual preference;
"   Protect and expand voting rights for people of color, women, immigrants, the elderly and students to safeguard fair democratic representation.

Co-Revolutionary Theory Becomes Practice: The Road Ahead

David Harvey [18] has written about a "co-revolutionary theory" of change. In this theory Harvey argues that anti-capitalist movements today must address "mental conceptions;" uses and abuses of nature; how to build real communities; workers relations to bosses; exploitation, oppression, and racism; and the relations between capital and the state. While a tall order, the co-revolutionary theory suggests the breadth of struggles that need to be embraced to bring about real revolution.

Harvey's work mirrors many analysts who address the deepening crises of capitalism and the spread of human misery everywhere. It is increasingly clear to vast majorities of people, despite media mystification, that the primary engine of destruction is global finance capitalism and political institutions that have increasingly become its instrumentality. Harvey's work parallels the insights of Naomi Klein, Joseph Stiglitz, Robert Reich, Noam Chomsky, and a broad array of economists, historians, trade unionists, peace and justice activists and thousands of bloggers and Facebook commentators.

Of course, these theorists could not have known the ways in which the connections between the co-revolutionary theory and practice would unfold. Most agreed that we are living through a global economic crisis in which wealth and power is increasingly concentrated in fewer and fewer hands (perhaps a global ruling class), and human misery, from joblessness, to hunger, to disease, to environmental devastation is spreading.

But history has shown that such misery can survive for long periods of time with little active resistance. Even though activists in labor, in communities of color, in anti-colonial/anti-neo-colonial settings are always organizing, their campaigns usually create little traction. Not so since 2011. Tunisians rose up against their oppressive government. Larger mobilizations occurred in Egypt. Protests spread to Yemen, Algeria, Oman, Bahrain, and Libya.

Assuming that working people, youth, women, and various professional groups would remain quiescent in the United States, right wing politicians saw the opportunity to radically transform American society by destroying public institutions and thereby shifting qualitatively more wealth from the majority to the minority. In Wisconsin, and later in Ohio, Indiana, and around the country a broad array of people began to publicly say "no," "enough is enough." Even those with criticisms of President Obama continued their mobilization to secure his reelection and the defeat of the rightwing.

The resistance in the Middle East has been about jobs, redistribution of wealth, limiting foreign financial penetration, and democracy. In the United States the issues are even more varied: the right of workers to collectively bargain, opposition to so-called Right-To-Work laws, beating back challenges to public education, raising demands for free access to health care including the defense of reproductive health care, and greater, not less, provision of jobs, livable wages, and retirement benefits.

Where do we go from here? I think "co-revolutionary theory" would answer "everywhere". Marxists are right to see the lives of people as anchored in their ability to produce and reproduce themselves, their families, and their communities. The right to a job at a living wage remains central to all the ferment. But in the twenty-first century this basic motivator for consciousness and action is more comprehensively and intimately connected to trade unions, education, health care, sustainable environments, opposition to racism and sexism, and peace. So all these motivations are part of the same struggle.

It is fascinating to observe that the reaction to economic ruling class and political elite efforts to turn back the clock on reforms gained over the last 75 years have sparked resistance and mobilization from across a whole array of movements and campaigns. And activists are beginning to make the connections between the struggles.

It is way too early to tell whether this round of ferment will lead to some victories for the people, even reformist ones. But as Harvey suggests, "An anti-capitalist political movement can start anywhere....The trick is to keep the political movement moving from one moment to another in mutually reinforcing ways."

Arab Spring to Moral Mondays

Between 2011 and the summer 2014, mass movements emerged projecting very different, even counter-hegemonic ideas about building a better world. Young people, workers, women, secularists, started going out in the streets in Tunisia, Egypt, Yemen, and Bahrain. They demanded democracy and economic justice. They began to mobilize in public spaces, such as schools, union halls, and mosques and churches. They communicated via cell phones and sent messages in silly shorthand sentences and (to me) incomprehensible letters. The sun and warmth of the Arab Spring blossomed.

In very different places economically, politically, and geographically, the bitter heartland of America, revolt was stirred up as well: Wisconsin, Ohio, Indiana, and Michigan for starters. Workers, students, women, political progressives, health care advocates, educators began to stand up and say no to the steamrolling right wing political machine, now not too different from the historic "centrist" consensus in U.S. politics. Like their comrades, the heartland radicals too haltingly began to suggest that another world is possible. And in 2013, Moral Mondays in North Carolina became visible and stimulated similar campaigns across the South, parts of the Midwest, and in selected states in the Southwest in 2014.

At the same time that revolt was spreading around the world, the United States carried out an assassination mission killing Osama bin Laden and encouraged a NATO-led war on the Gaddafi family dictatorship in Libya and is now in the process of resuming interventions in Iraq, Syria, Ukraine, and Venezuela, and across the African continent. At home, stories about the need for austerity programs to reduce the federal deficit fill the air waves and state legislatures controlled by the Tea Party and its allies adopt anti-worker, anti-women, anti-Black, and anti-environmental policies. For most US politicians, the country's problems are not about capitalism or neo-liberal economic policies. Many of these claim that problems stem from too much government.

The forces of ideological hegemony say we need to keep our guard up and be prepared to kill those who threaten us or who are claimed to be threats. Criminal justice systems and norms against violence are to be ignored. At home we must challenge the idea that political institutions, government, must serve the needs of the people.

However, recent evidence suggests that resistance is growing all across the globe. The new precariat are seemingly playing a major role in the new resistance, demanding changes in the distribution of wealth and income, expanding access to medical care and education, jobs, and political empowerment. Whether the mobilizations will lead to a renewed socialist left-left unity- committed to building a new social order, a non-capitalist one, remains to be seen.

Notes

[1] Wayne Ellwood, The No-Nonsense Guide to Globalization, New York: Verso, 2002.
[2] Harry Targ, Challenging Late Capitalism, Neo-Liberal Globalization and Militarism: Building a Progressive Majority, Chicago: Changemaker, 2006. William K. Tabb, Economic Governance in the Age of Globalization, New York: Columbia, 2004.Manfred B. Steger, Globalization, A Very Short Introduction, New York: oxford, 2009.
[3] Thomas Friedman, Lexus and the Olive Tree, New York: Anchor, 2000.
[4] Ellen Meiksins Wood, "Capitalism, Globalization, and Epochal Shifts: An Exchange," Monthly Review, February, 1997, 21-32.
[5] Harry Targ, Challenging Late Capitalism, Neo-Liberal Globalization, and Militarism: Building a Progressive Majority, 35-52.Sarah Anderson, John Cavanagh, and Thea Lee, Field Guide to the Global Economy, New York: The New Press, 2005.
[6] William I. Robinson, A Theory of Global Capitalism: Production, Class,

and State in a Transnational World, Washington: Johns Hopkins, 2004. Jerry Harris, The Dialectics of Globalization: Economic and Political Conflict in a Transnational World, London: Cambridge Scholars Publishing, 2008.

[7] United Nations, Department of Economic and Social Affairs, "The 2005 Report on the World Social Situation: The Inequality Predicament," 2005.

[8] International Labor Organization, "Economic Growth Leaves Jobs Behind," ilo.org, January 21, 2014.

[9] Guy Standing, The Precariat: The New Dangerous Class, Bloomsbury, New York, 2012.

[10] University of Sydney, "The Precariat: the New Dangerous Class," Asian Correspondent.com, February 9, 2012.

[11] Zahara Heckscher, "Long Before Seattle: Historical Resistance to Economic Globalization," in Robin Broad ed. Global Backlash: Citizen Initiatives for a Just World Economy, Lanham, Maryland: Rowman and Littlefield, 2002, 86-92.

[12] Naomi Klein, "A Fete for the End of the End of History," The Nation, March 19, 2001.

[13] Action Center for Justice, "June 27-July1 US Social Forum in Atlanta," www.charlotteaction.blogspot.com/2007/06/june-27-july-1-us-social-forum-in.html

[14] US Social Forum, "US Social Forum 2010: Vision and Goals," www.ussocialforum.net/esnode/4

[15] Isabel Ortiz, Sara Burke, Mohamed Berrada, Hernan Cortes. World Protests 2006-2013, Friedrich Ebert Stiftung, New York Office, September, 2013.

[17] Vijay Prashad, "Interview," MRZine, Monthly Review.org, February 4, 2011.

[18] David Harvey, The Enigma of Capital and the Crises of Capitalism, New York: Oxford, 2011.

Harry Targ teaches Political Science at Purdue University and is a member of the National Executive Committee CCDS. This paper was presented at the "Moving Beyond Capitalism Conference", Center for Global Justice, San Miguel de Allende, Mexico, July 29-August 5, 2014.

New Developments In Labor: The Fight Against Racism, Injustice & Austerity

By Paul Krehbiel

Political and economic pundits have been announcing the steady death spiral of the labor movement for years. The markers were there: the dramatic loss of union members, cuts in pay and benefits, the off-shoring of more jobs, high unemployment, growing part-time and precarious work, and more.

Then, on April 24, 2015, over 60,000 fast food workers and other low paid employees went on strike in over 200 cities and towns across the country demanding $15 an hour and a union. Among them were low paid workers from Walmart, home health care aides, activists in the Black Lives Matter movement, child care workers, adjunct professors, and many more from widely varied fields.

That doesn't mean that labor's troubles are over and is on the road to recovery. Much more needs to be done. But the fast food and WalMart strikes on April 15, 2014 and April 15, 2015 and many other labor initiatives, including other strikes and political organizing, signal a renewed fighting spirit by the working-class. This has been remarkable for many reasons.

Unions in the US and in most countries have been under a withering attack by employers, the global capitalist elite, and their right-wing allies for the past 30-40 years. The assault has taken a toll. In the mid-1950s the percentage of the US workforce organized into unions was 35%. Today that number is 11%. In the US, entire industries that were formerly heavily unionized, like steel production, are mostly gone from the US landscape. Threats of more closures, more off-shoring of jobs, more concessions rammed down workers throats, more cuts in social services, more workers pushed into part-time and precarious work, more workers forced into the ranks of the long-term unemployed and the forever unemployed is the name of the game. That is not only happening in the US, but with some exceptions, across the entire globe. Capitalism has won and labor has been vanquished, claim the pundits and many labor and economic experts, echoing the crowing of the elites in the corporate and banking world.

The fast food workers strikes and demonstrations are the latest and most dramatic refutation of this in the recent period. But something else is going on below the public radar. Unions are fighting back in a myriad of ways. One way is that they are quietly reaching out to other allies in working-class communities, and among social justice movements which are also predominately working-class. Labor's goal is to build alliances of mutual support. The results have often been good, sometimes even stunning, showing that such synergy creates a power that is considerably greater than the sum of its parts. Labor has built these alliances before, most notably during the union organizing drives of the 1930s and 1940s initiated by the Congress of Industrial Organization (CIO). That hugely successful drive brought millions of industrial workers into unions, changing the balance of power between capital and labor.

The Left as a Driving Force

A driving force in organizing the CIO was the political left; the largest organization in that left-wing movement was the Communist Party. Capital was still in charge, but it was weakened, while workers made badly needed gains. The anti-communist Cold War of the 1950s drove most, but not all, of the progressives, leftists, Communists and Socialists out of the labor movement, and severed labor's alliances with community and social justice organizations and movements. Some of those alliances were rebuilt, but not on the scale and breadth we are seeing today, in part because of the plethora of social justice organizations and issue campaigns that exist today. That is the key new development in the labor movement, and it holds much promise for the revitalization of the union movement and the political left in our country.

As this labor-community-social justice alliance grows, we can begin to see instead of just 13 million union members, 30-40 million working-class people working together in support of both social justice issues and labor union causes. That is tremendous political and union power. Many of the social justice, community, and labor campaigns today include housing, health care, education, civil rights, democracy, pollution and climate change, students and youth, seniors, the LGBT community, affordable prices, good wages, Social Security, Medicare, and many others. While most of the activists and supporters of these issue campaigns are currently not in unions they have many of the same concerns and issues as union workers. This process is uneven, but it is developing and progressing. Some of the alliances are being made in what many might think are unlikely places and around unlikely issues. But as union and non-union workers get to know and respect each other, there will be a whole new field of non-union workers who will become interested in joining a union.

Fighting Racism

Labor united with the Civil Rights movement in the past and both groups made gains. Today, unknown to the general public, the labor movement is linking up with and assisting the Black Lives Matter movement.

On August 14, 2014, Michael Brown, an unarmed Black teenager, was shot and killed by a white police officer, Darren Wilson, in Ferguson, Missouri. This, one in a series of white police officers shooting unarmed Blacks, some in the back, sparked an outrage in Ferguson and across the country. Massive demonstrations, many led by Black youth while working with other races, filled the streets of Ferguson and scores of other cities and towns across the country. Union leaders and union members joined, along with many other community organizations and residents, to speak out and protest against these murders. Some union leaders are meeting with Black and community leaders to find solutions to these serious problems. The mass corporate-controlled media, has for the most part, said little about this grassroots organizing.

Richard Trumka, president of the 13-million member AFL-CIO, spoke at the Missouri AFL-CIO Convention in St. Louis on September 15, 2014, one month after Michael Brown's murder. He began by saying that he was going to stray from his usual convention speech to talk about something that may be difficult to talk about, but must be talked about. As his speech unfolded, it was clear that he was talking to all the leaders present, and especially the white union leaders in the room.

I"'m talking about race in America and what it means for our communities, our movement and our nation.

"Because the reality is that while a young man named Michael Brown died just a short distance from us in Ferguson, from gunshot wounds from a police officer, other young men of color have died and will die in similar circumstances, in communities all across this country.

"It happened here but it could have happened – does happen – anywhere in America. Because the reality is we still have racism in America.

"Now, some people might ask me why our labor movement should be involved in all that has happened since the tragic death of Michael Brown in Ferguson. And I want to answer that question directly. How can we not be involved?"

Trumka went on to explain that Michael Brown's mother is a union member, and so is Darren Wilson. "Union member's lives have been profoundly damaged in ways that can't be fixed." He said that there must be an open discussion about racism in society, including in the union movement. He said that "We must take responsibility for the past. Racism is part of our inheritance as Americans." He talked about terrible murders that took place in St. Louis in 1917. Powerful corporations replaced white strikers with African American workers from Mississippi, promising them higher wages than what they were making sharecropping. The corporations didn't tell them they were going to be used as strike-breakers. When they arrived in St. Louis, they were attacked by the white strikers and many African American men, women and children were killed. Trumka quoted Eugene Debs, the founder of the National Railway Union then and a leader of the Socialist Party, that the St. Louis Massacre was "a foul blot on the American labor movement."

Trumka said, "Remember we are here today because labor leaders like A. Philip Randolph and Walter Reuther showed us there was a better way, not just for our unions, but for our country." He continued by saying that if the labor movement is going to be a force for good we must eliminate racism. He said he never had to worry when his son went out at night "that he might be stopped, shot by a police officer. But for millions of mothers and fathers of young African American men and boys, men just like my son...it is a constant fear, a constant fear."

He continued: "This is not somebody else's problem. This is the reality of life for millions of our brothers and sisters. And so it is our problem. That is what solidarity means." Toward the end of his speech, he said: "We need to be out in our communities – building larger working-class political alliances. That's how we break the isolation. That's how we fight racism. That's how we win."

On November 24, 2014 a Grand Jury in Missouri failed to issue an indictment of Darren Wilson. Protests escalated. In Ferguson, and some other cities, police responded with a display of military weapons, tear gas, rubber bullets, abuse and arrests of demonstrators. In Ferguson, the police displayed a sniper's tripod assault rifle, just like in the movie, American Sniper.

Immediate protest demonstrations of over ten thousand people took place in Baltimore, Newark, Providence, Raleigh and Durham (North Carolina), Atlanta, Syracuse, Camden, Cleveland, Milwaukee, Chicago, Los Angeles, Oakland, Seattle and many other cities and towns, with over 1,000 in New York City, 3,000 in Atlanta, 1,000 in Philadelphia, and 1,000 in St. Louis. Over 50 demonstrators were arrested in Boston. Led predominately by Black youth, these demonstrations were multi-racial and comprised of union members, students, the faith community and people from many other walks of life.

Fighting Injustices

In some cities, the labor movement played the leading role in organizing protests. In Camden, New Jersey, three local unions of the Communication Workers of America spearheaded the organization of the rally there. CWA Local 1084 President George Jackson, said, "We're not just about union and contracts; we are about children, and the community, and schools and education, and against young men being shot down. We're about civil rights. We need some kind of legislation for policing. We need to press our legislators." The CWA handed out T-shirts, signs and buttons demanding "Justice for Michael Brown." There are the beginnings of breaks in the ranks of the police nation-wide. That is a good start, even though it's tepid. The current Camden County chief of police, Scott Thomson, criticized how the police in Ferguson handled the demonstrators because the police showed "the absence of a meaningful relationship between that community and the police."

In Ferguson, large numbers of union members joined the protest marches after the Grand Jury decision not to indict Darren Wilson. Nicholas James, an SEIU representative, said there "were purple (SEIU) shirts donned by my union members, before me and after me. SEIU banners were being carried, and purple (SEIU's color) bracelets were everywhere I looked. I could not have been prouder."

National union leaders spoke out against the killing of Michael Brown and other Black men murdered by white police officers, and in support of the protest demonstration in Ferguson and across the country. Their members heard these statements, but few statements were published in the national mass media. The national office of the Communications Workers of America issued a press statement that said in part: "By declining to indict Officer Darren Wilson on the shooting of Michael Brown, the legal system has failed... civil rights (have been) violated."

Joe Hansen, national president of the United Food and Commercial Workers said: "The simple truth is that there are too many Michael Browns in America needlessly having their lives cut short and we in the labor movement have a responsibility to take action."

Mark Esters, from the Coalition of Black Trade Unionists, said: "We in the labor movement understand the meaning of struggle for economic, racial and social justice. We salute our youth who put their lives on the frontline..."

AFL-CIO leader Rich Trumka denounced the injustice and said that labor was "working with local community organizations to address issues of racial and economic inequality that surround Ferguson and so many other communities like it."

Mary Kay Henry, president of the 2-million member Service Employees International Union (SEIU), said the grand jury's decision "deepens those wounds and amplifies even more the disproportionate and disparate injustices experienced by communities of color. The Department of Justice must prioritize the investigation into the murder of Michael Brown."

Fast Food Workers

While many of the protests at fast food restaurants were undertaken by the fast food workers on their own, they have sought and received assistance from the labor movement. Service Employees International Union (SEIU) is supporting the fast food workers, and the United Food and Commercial Workers (UFCW) is supporting the Walmart workers. What is especially important is that these workers movements have also received support from community organizations, and the low wage workers have expressed support for community issues. When fast food workers went out on nation-wide strikes in cities across the country in 2014 and on April 15, 2015 to demand $15 an hour and a union, many also carried signs in support of the protests in Ferguson. I was at a rally of fast food workers outside a downtown McDonald's restaurant in Los Angeles in September of 2014 and saw signs demanding justice for Michael Brown and in support of the Black Lives Matter movement.

The burgeoning alliance between the Black Lives Matter movement, fast food workers organizing campaign, and SEIU, is being joined by other organizations, including the Moral Monday movement, organized to fight cutbacks, austerity, and the rightwing government in North Carolina. The Moral Monday movement is helping the fast food workers, and fast food workers have attended protests of the Moral Monday movement. Moral Mondays has since spread to other states in the south and into the mid-west, such as in Indiana. All these groups met to coordinate support for the fast food workers strikes and demonstrations on April 15, 2015 across the country. McDonald's, the largest fast food restaurant in the US and the world, has been targeted by the fast food workers, and they've won some initial improvements.

On April 1, 2015, McDonald's restaurants announced that it would raise pay for 90,000 of its workers in company run stores but not in the more numerous "franchise" stores," by $1 an hour. That would raise the pay for some to near $10 an hour, though lower paid workers will get less. The McDonald workers responded by saying thanks, but we want $15 and a union for all workers. McDonald's made $5.5 billion in profit in 2013. The company could pay $15 an hour to all its workers, though top executives such as President and CEO Donald Thompson may have to cut his total compensation which was $9.5 million in 2013. The average McDonald's worker earns $8.25 an hour. Most fast food workers earn in that range. Fast food workers are so poorly paid that 52% are on public assistance. There are over 500,000 McDonald's workers in the US, and 1.9 million world-wide.

McDonald's workers in other countries have joined the campaign. Some McDonald's workers in Europe have organized unions at McDonald's stores and have doubled and tripled their wages and benefits. Workers can make $45,000 a year in Denmark. The workers in different countries are working to help each other through channels that their respective unions have established to give support to each other.

Walmart workers also are organizing for $15 an hour and a union. Walmart made $16 billion in profit in 2013 and is the top earning company in the US. Walmart employs 1.4 million workers in the US, 1% of the entire 140 million US workforce. World-wide, Walmart employs 2.1 million workers.

New Alliances

There are other supporters of this campaign to raise the wages of low paid workers. The National Gay and Lesbian Task Force encouraged the LGBT community to join the fight for a" living wage" since many LGBT (Lesbian, Gay, Bisexual, Transgender) people are also locked into low wage jobs, including at fast food restaurants and at Walmart. The "$15 an hour and a union" movement begun among fast food workers and Walmart workers will now spread to other low wage industries via the LGBT community. This is the kind of movement that can grow exponentially.

There are a lot of other examples of unions and social justice movements working together. Some have formed alliances on their own; others have been encouraged by the national AFL-CIO since its National Convention in Los Angeles in October 2013 where it launched a national program to reach out to potential community partners.

One example is the People's Climate March, held in New York City on September 21, 2014. Over 1,500 organizations endorsed the march, a coalition of environmentalists, community, religious, women's, labor, civil rights groups, and many others. An estimated 400,000 people took part in the march and rally in conjunction with the United Nations Climate Summit meeting. This included over 10,000 unionists from 70 unions.

George Miranda, President of the Teamsters Joint Council 16 in New York, and an International Vice President of the Teamsters, said "for years, many of us in the labor movement sat back while the environmentalists fought for a safe planet for the rest of us. For me, it brings to mind an old union saying: 'stand together, or fall apart.' More and more I see the climate fight as my fight too. Many of my union brothers and sisters feel the same. Drought, rising sea levels, and superstorms like Hurricane Sandy (that hit New York) have shown us that climate change is here, and the people hardest hit are the workers...I have found strong friends in the environmental movement and we are working together to protect workers and the environment at the same time."

Some of the participating unions included the National Nurses United, Communication Workers of America, Amalgamated Transit Union, National Education Association, and regional and local union bodies such as the Connecticut AFL-CIO, Albany County Central Federation of Labor, AFL-CIO, United Teachers of Los Angeles. They were joined by 350.org, Physicians for Social Responsibility, NAACP, MoveOn.org, National Audubon Society, Buddhist Association of America, and some socialist organizations including the Committees of Correspondence for Democracy and Socialism.

Environmental and labor groups also worked on specific struggles together. Oil refinery workers went out on a national strike February 1, 2015 at 11 oil refineries in Texas, Kentucky, Washington, Ohio, Indiana, and California. The workers, members of the United Steelworkers, went on strike over health hazards to themselves and the surrounding communities from toxic chemicals from the refineries, not money. A number of environmental groups supported the striking workers, including the Sierra Club, the largest with 2.4 million members. Sierra Club Executive Director, Michael Brune, said: "The Sierra Club and the United Steelworkers co-founded the BlueGreen Alliance and have jointly spoken out to make it clear that the health and safety of workers and communities and the protection of the environment are inextricably linked." Other unions in the BlueGreen Alliance include SEIU, CWA, UFCW, UAW, Utility Workers, and other environmental groups such as the Union of Concerned Scientists.

Other social justice issues that labor is involved in with other organizations include the campaign for improved Medicare for All. The Labor

Campaign for Single-Payer Healthcare, comprised of leaders from over 50 unions and labor bodies, met with two other national single-payer community-based organizations in Oakland, California, August 22-24, 2014 to develop strategies to advance this campaign.

During the war on Iraq, trade unionists from many unions formed US Labor Against the War (USLAW) and joined the largest peace coalition in the country, United for Peace and Justice, to work with others to bring an end to the war. USLAW worked especially close with military families and veterans, such as Iraq Veterans Against the War, and brought Iraqi labor leaders to the US to meet with their union counterparts. Today, a major focus is to work with other organizations to shift money from the bloated military budget to fund social needs to replenish government coffers after the massive cuts that were imposed in the ongoing austerity drive by neoliberals from the capitalist elite and their politicians.

Unions Fight Austerity

Unions have been fighting the austerity drive with mixed success. Where they have built strong alliances and developed a smart plan that involved large numbers of people, both union and community, they have had greater success. One of the early anti-austerity campaigns took place in Los Angeles County in 2002 when a budget shortfall led County Supervisors to announce the closing of most public community clinics and two of the county's six public hospitals. SEIU Local 660 (now Local 721), representing 20,000 health care workers in Los Angeles County (and 30,000 in other county departments), developed a plan with input from rank-and-file members, union staff representatives, and community organizations to stop the facility closings and health service curtailments.

I worked for SEIU Local 660 then and was involved in this campaign. The county health facilities serve primarily residents without health insurance who are predominately low income, and overwhelmingly Latino including a significant number of immigrants. The union worked with Democratic allies on the Board of Supervisors to develop a plan. They decided to put a measure on the November ballot to slightly raise property taxes to cover the short fall in the health budget. A number of rank-and-file leaders and union staff leaders urged raising taxes slightly on the very wealthy to pay for the shortfall, but the union leaders and Supervisors wanted to stay with the property tax increase.

Fortunately it was a small increase, but we still had to convince voters to vote for it, since most of them did not use the county health system. The only way was to find something in the county health system that the general public did use, and that was the Trauma Network. This Network is comprised of county hospitals and private hospitals which are specially equipped to handle trauma cases, such as serious auto accidents, and natural disasters like earthquakes, floods and fires. The message for the campaign was that if Los Angeles County voters don't vote for a slight increase in their property taxes two county hospitals would close and the Trauma Network would collapse. This was not a campaign threat to scare voters. It was true because cutbacks in the healthcare system in previous years seriously weakened the Trauma Network.

The union mobilized hundreds of members to work on this campaign largely through the union's Stewards Councils. One steward, Lavon Luster, an ambulance driver for the county Department of Health Services, was also youth pastor for his church in South Central Los Angeles. Through his church work, and with other youth pastors in many other churches throughout central Los Angeles, Luster organized a team of pastors and church youth to speak in area churches and pass out literature to support Measure B.

This was just one of many examples of union members having contacts with community organizations that were brought into the campaign for Measure B. Measure B passed on election day, one of the first major rejections of the neoliberal agenda. It passed because SEIU Local 660 developed a smart campaign plan and built a broad union-community coalition to successfully carry out that plan. This is another example of a union having influence way beyond its size. Good functioning unions, with good internal democracy and member empowerment, and guided by the labor adage "An injury to one is an injury to all," are schools of socialism. Good functioning Stewards Councils greatly empower members and function along socialist lines, becoming building blocks in creating strands of socialism within the fabric of a capitalist society.

In early 2011, right-wing Republican Governor of Wisconsin, Scott Walker, rammed through the Republican-dominated state legislature a bill to strip public sector unions in Wisconsin of their bargaining rights. Led by a union of low paid teaching assistants and adjunct professors at the university, the union movement joined together to occupy the state capitol in Madison to protest this anti-worker law.

The union group also had the support of the Madison police union, and large numbers of community groups who came to the capital to support the workers. Unfortunately, they were not able to reverse this law, and failed to recall Governor Walker in a special election. One reason was that Walker outspent his democratic rival by 2-1 with much financial and other help from the right-wing Koch brothers of Koch Industries. But thousands of union workers and community members learned important lessons to help them in future struggles. One was building labor-community alliances.

In Ohio, another right-wing governor, John Kasich, passed an anti-labor bill, SB 5, in the state legislature in 2011 that would curb bargaining rights for 350,000 unionized public workers. Through their unions, and working with allies in the community, pro-labor activists collected enough signatures to put a measure on the ballot to rescind SB 5. They mobilized thousands of supporters and won.

Lessons From Abroad

The best example of workers organizing against austerity and right-wing political leaders was the mass movement that Greek unions undertook to stop the deep cuts in jobs and social services by European and global capitalist financial institutions. Greek unions organized a series of general strikes to protest the cutbacks, crippling the economy and causing big losses to Greek and European capitalist corporations. The Greek labor movement helped mobilize other sectors of society to oppose these harmful policies. This movement laid the political groundwork for the election of the left-wing, anti-austerity party Syriza to national office in January 2015.

Workers in the US and our unions have things to learn from the Greek labor movement. Our US labor movement must step up serious discussions and plans for more labor actions of all kinds, including general strikes (like the Wisconsin labor movement considered in 2011), and more joint activity with community organizations and social justice organizations to fight austerity everywhere, and to strengthen the Black Lives Matter movement, the drive for a $15 minimum wage and a union, and all other labor rights and social justice issues.

As long as capitalism rules, people will continually have these problems: racism, injustice, inequality, exploitation, austerity and war. The key is to empower people at the grassroots, build large democratic alliances with as many organizations and constituencies who agree on a common program to stop these abuses as possible. We must win immediate reforms to make improvements for the working-class as a whole and especially the most oppressed parts of it, and use these building blocks to weaken the exploitation and abuses of the capitalist elite and to create a fairer, more human and just society, socialism. To do this we must win over the majority of the people.

Paul Krehbiel is a former union auto worker, local union president, and chief negotiator for 5,000 Registered Nurses in Los Angeles County in the 2000s and member of SEIU Local 660 (now 721). He is a member of Labor United for Universal Healthcare, and the National Coordinating Committee of CCDS.

Growers Move to Gut California's Farm Labor Law

By David Bacon

When hundreds of people marched to the Los Angeles City Council last October, urging it to pass a resolution supporting a farm worker union fight taking place in California's San Joaquin Valley, hardly anyone had ever heard the name of the company involved. That may not be the case much longer. Gerawan Farming, one of the country's largest growers, with 5,000 people picking its grapes and peaches, is challenging the California law that makes farm workers' union rights enforceable. Lining up behind Gerawan are national anti-union think tanks. What began as a local struggle by one grower family to avoid a union contract is getting bigger, and the stakes are getting much higher.

The Gerawan workers got the City Council's support and, on February 10, the Los Angeles Unified School District Board of Education passed a resolution that went beyond just an encouraging statement. The LAUSD purchases Gerawan's Prima label peaches and grapes through suppliers for 1,270 schools and 907,000 students. The LAUSD's resolution, proposed by board member Steve Zimmer, requires the district to verify that Gerawan Farming is abiding by state labor laws, "and to immediately implement the agreement issued by the neutral mediator and the state of California."

Verifying compliance, however, may not be easy. In mid-March a hearing on Gerawan's violations of the Agricultural Labor Relations Act (ALRA) ended after 104 days of testimony by 130 witnesses. According to the Agricultural Labor Relations' Board's general counsel, Sylvia Torres-Guillén, and its regional director in Visalia, Silas Shawver, Gerawan mounted an intense campaign against the United Farm Workers after the union requested bargaining in October 2012. According to the board, Gerawan sought to "undermine the UFW's status as its employees' bargaining representative; to turn its employees against the union; to

promote decertification of the UFW; and to prevent the UFW from ever representing its employees under a collective bargaining agreement."

The conflict at Gerawan Farming has been building for 26 years. In 1990 over a thousand workers voted in a union election in its fields near Madera, in the San Joaquin Valley, choosing the United Farm Workers. The company was not neutral towards its workers' efforts to organize, however. After the 1990 election the ALRB issued two complaints against the company - for laying off workers in 32 crews to eliminate them from the voting list, and for firing one crew because workers were UFW supporters. A state hearing officer found the company guilty of tearing down six labor camps to intimidate them.

Five years after that election, having exhausted legal efforts to overturn it, Mike Gerawan finally sat down with UFW representatives. Instead of negotiating, however, he told them: "I don't want the union and I don't need the union." That ended bargaining before it even started. Over the next 17 years, with no contract, Gerawan Farming grew to become one of the nation's largest growers, exporting its Prima label fruit globally.

Hardball tactics towards unions in the fields have been typical of California growers. Although the Agricultural Labor Relations Act in 1975 gave farm workers the right to vote for unions, the law had no teeth to force unwilling growers to negotiate contracts afterwards. According to UC Davis professor Philip Martin, workers were unable to win agreements in 243 of 428 farms where they'd voted for the UFW between 1975 and 2002.

Federal law has never covered farm workers. Outside of California, no state has a law giving farm workers a legal process for recognition and bargaining. The few union agreements that exist in other states are the products of long campaigns and boycotts. As a result, less than one percent of the nation's farm workers have union contracts. Wages and conditions in farm labor are worse than in almost any other occupation.

In 2002, however, California's legislature passed two bills that amended the original law. Today the ALRA allows a union to ask for a mediator if a grower won't reach agreement on a first-time contract. Once the Board adopts the mediator's report it becomes a contract. The process is called mandatory mediation. Growers challenged this process and lost at the state court of appeals in 2006. The UFW has since used the law to negotiate contracts at several large employers, covering about 3000 workers.

In 2012 the UFW made another demand for bargaining at Gerawan. This time, according to the labor board, the company unleashed a sophisticated drive, not just against the union but against the law itself. In that effort, it's acquired the help of some of the country's most conservative advocacy groups and think tanks. Losing mandatory mediation would be devastating to the UFW. No real union can survive indefinitely without being able to win contracts, and through them, gain members and improve wages and conditions.

A Dirty Election

The UFW says it continued working with Gerawan workers to improve conditions during the 17-year hiatus between 1995 and 2012. According to Gerawan's publicist, Erin Shaw, "The UFW abandoned Gerawan employees without ever negotiating a collective bargaining agreement."

Nevertheless, the UFW renewed its bargaining demand in October 2012, and union workers chose a negotiating committee. This time the company sat down at the bargaining table - from January to July of 2013. But when bargaining went nowhere, the union filed for mandatory mediation. Gerawan still claims there is no negotiated agreement. But according to UFW negotiating committee member Agustin Rodriguez, "We negotiated a contract. The company refuses to implement it."

Gerawan did not want about 2000 workers hired through labor contractors covered by any agreement. Those workers are paid less than the company's own employees. The company sought to keep a medical plan that only 13 of its workers could afford, Rodriguez says. "In the company rulebook," he told Capital and Main, "they can fire you with or without a reason. With the union, they can only fire you for just cause.

This is what the company doesn't want. It has power right now and it doesn't want to lose it."

A key allegation in the ALRB complaint charges Gerawan Farming with manipulating wages to keep the union out. The company boasts it pays $11.00/hour -- $2 above the state minimum -- and says it shows workers are better off without a union. Fifteen-year employee Severino Salas believes, however, "it's the pressure from the union" that got the company to raise wages. "They're not giving us $11 for nothing," adds Rodriguez. "Until recently they'd accuse whole crews of not working fast enough and fire them."

In June 2013, while bargaining was going on, Gerawan rehired Silvia Lopez, a previous employee whose boyfriend was a company supervisor, and whose daughter and son-in-law also work there. Lopez "began her involvement in anti-union activities at Gerawan before she started working for the company," according to the ALRB. Almost immediately she became a client of Paul Bauer, a lawyer for a Fresno firm representing employers in labor disputes.

Decertification Campaign

Lopez began to collect signatures on a petition for a decertification election to get rid of the UFW. Companies can't assist such efforts, but Lopez and her friends collected signatures during work hours, and rarely even worked a full day picking grapes. The company set up a supportive website, helpfarmworkers.com, that announces, "This website is [the workers'] effort to insure that their voices are heard in Sacramento, and they get to make their own decision."

Salas charges foremen told workers the company would uproot trees and vines if the union came in. "They'd just plant almonds and pistachios that don't need many workers. People were afraid to support the union, even though they wanted it, for fear of losing their jobs," he recalls.

In August 2013 Dan Gerawan invited Lopez and her friends to go with him to Sacramento, to testify against a bill that would have strengthened mandatory mediation. On September 18, as the mediator prepared to issue his report, Lopez turned in her petitions. Shawver and his staff compared the signatures to the employee list and found there weren't enough.

By then, Sylvia Lopez had an additional lawyer, Anthony Raimondo, who also represents Gerawan's two largest labor contractors, Sunshine Agricultural Services and R&T Grafting Labor. He asked for more time, and signature collection went into overdrive. Of the additional signatures he turned in, an exhaustive investigation found at least 100 were forged, allegedly from workers employed by Raimondo's contractor clients. The ALRB found many foremen and forewomen had participated in collecting signatures. In just one case, "after explaining the petition and sending the employees to work, [supervisor] Sonia Martinez went row by row and provided the employees in her crew with the signature sheet," according to the ALRB complaint. The decertification petition was dismissed.

A second decertification campaign was immediately launched. On September 27 the company gave time off to hundreds of workers, to leave their crews and go to Visalia to demonstrate outside the ALRB office. According to the ALRB, the following Monday supervisors shut down work entirely, blocked entry to the fields and packing sheds, handed out petitions and demanded that workers sign. A statement by Gerawan claims "1,500 workers walked out of the fields" and describes this as "the largest ever seen in California's agricultural industry."

Two days later the California Grape and Tree Fruit League, a grower organization, supplied busses, food and anti-union tee-shirts to Gerawan workers, taking them to Sacramento to lobby for decertification. A lawyer at McCormick Barstow LLP (Raimundo's Fresno law firm at the time) ordered four busses and snacks, costing $6,366, from Classic Charter, listing Sylvia Lopez as the contact person.

That order was paid with the credit card of Barry Bedwell, president of the California Grape and Tree Fruit League. His card statement includes a charge for a similar charter for $3,466. He additionally paid $3512.70 for burritos, and bought 1,170 tee-shirts for the demonstrations. In total he spent $19,234.70. The League's board of directors includes Gerawan vice-president George Nikolich along with some of the biggest family names in California agriculture: Giumarra, Pandol, Bagdasarian, Zaninovich and others.

Media Campaign

Meanwhile a media campaign produced TV and newspaper stories alleging workers were being denied the right to vote in a decertification election. The labor board in Sacramento, whose appointed members have final say over the agency's decisions, seesawed back and forth.

First it delayed approving the contract drawn up by the mediator.

But then Shawver and Torres-Guillén rejected the second petition as well. When the company appealed, the labor board ordered them to conduct the decertification election anyway, despite the charges of company interference.

Workers voted on November 5, 2013. Their votes were impounded, however. Legally, they cannot be counted unless an investigation concludes the company had nothing to do with organizing the decertification campaign.

After the election, the ALRB finally approved the mediator's contract. Gerawan Farming refused to implement it, and Torres-Guillen formally charged the company with violating the mandatory mediation law.

Gerawan then asked a judge at the state court of appeals in Fresno to declare mandatory mediation unconstitutional, overturning the 2006 decision upholding it. Joining Gerawan were the Western Growers Association, the California Farm Bureau Federation and the California Grape and Tree Fruit League (now the California Fresh Fruit Association). Even Lopez and Raimondo filed an amicus brief.

A Gerawan statement claims, "We support [workers'] right to choose, but the ALRB staff and the UFW do not. Our sole message to our employees has never wavered: 'We want what you want.' There is now only one correct and just solution to ensure employees' rights are protected. Count the ballots."

According to veteran labor lawyer David Rosenfeld, who teaches law at the University of California's Boalt Hall Law School, "Gerawan has all the money in the world, and doesn't lose anything by appealing. In the meantime, they can delay implementing the contract for at least a couple of years." The company's problem, he believes, is that the state Supreme Court is generally favorable to workers' issues.

Conservative Groups Gather Around Gerawan

As this fight unfolds national anti-union organizations are moving in. The Center for Constitutional Jurisprudence joined the appeals case. This far-right legal institute holds that "The right to acquire, protect, and enjoy property was considered to be one of the fundamental, inalienable natural rights of mankind." In recent years the Center has joined the Harris v. Quinn suit against the Service Employees International Union in Illinois, sued the California Labor Commissioner on behalf of employers, argued for Hobby Lobby Stores against birth control, and supported the initiative to end affirmative action in Michigan.

Much of the San Joaquin Valley is conservative Republican territory. In "The Perfect Fruit," author Chip Brantley quotes Ray Gerawan: "My philosophy is survival of the fittest," he says. "In this family, we're real big on free enterprise." He says his ambition is "to put my competitors out of business ... because that makes us all stronger."

The Gerawan's local congressman, Devin Nunes, is a grower who criticized President Obama for opposing the use of torture. Republican Kevin McCarthy is the House Majority Leader representing neighboring Bakersfield. Both are allies of Grover Norquist's Americans for Tax Reform (ATR), a key opponent of mandatory mediation funded by Karl Rove's Crossroads GPS and the Koch brothers, among other conservative sources.

The Center for Worker Freedom, headquartered in ATR offices in Washington DC, publicized the pro-decertification demonstration outside the Visalia ALRB office. The Center's director, Matt Patterson, wrote an editorial for Forbes.com, extolling Lopez and charging, "farm workers in California's Central Valley are finding their civil liberties stripped from them today - by a government agency ... [that] wants to force the union on Gerawan until the election is 'investigated'." Last year Patterson bought billboards to attack the United Auto Workers at the new Volkswagen plant in Chattanooga, Tennessee. Copying the same strategy, the Center then bought billboards in Sacramento attacking the UFW and the ALRB.

This year the Gerawan's local state assembly member, Republican Jim Patterson of Fresno, introduced AB 1389. It would allow groups like Sylvia Lopez and her friends to inject themselves into mandatory mediation proceedings on the same basis as the union's elected negotiating committee. Further, it would allow growers to decertify unions that "abandon" workers for three years, an obvious reference to Gerawan. Both measures would make mandatory mediation essentially unworkable.

When the Gerawans are criticized, they react with hardball tactics. When Berkeley passed a resolution like Los Angeles', it got a swift and threatening response. Company attorney David Schwarz wrote a four-page letter to its city council. "Republication of libelous statements," he fumed, "whether in newsletters, press releases, constituent updates, or speeches outside the legislative chamber, is not immunized from liability..." Katy Grimes, who writes for the Watchdog Wire blog (a project of the pro-free-market Franklin Center for Government and Public Integrity), called the resolution's authors "liberal busybodies."

Last June former California Supreme Court Justice Cruz Reynoso coauthored an op-ed piece with UFW President Arturo Rodriguez, urging the company to negotiate with its workers. Reynoso was formerly director of California Rural Legal Assistance, the state's legal advocacy organization for farm workers. In 1981 Jerry Brown, in his first stint as governor, appointed him to the state Supreme Court. In 1986 growers and rightwing Republicans spent $7 million to recall him and two other justices.

After seeing Reynoso's op-ed, Dan Gerawan sent him a threatening letter. At the end of eight pages it demanded "that you disavow authorship of the article. If you refuse to do so, then we ask that you correct the false and misleading statements made in the article, and retract these defamatory statements. The retraction must be complete and unequivocal." Reynoso politely refused. "I respectfully decline to disavow authorship nor do I find any statements to be false, misleading or defamatory," he countered.

Despite the threats and name-calling city councils in New York City and Washington D.C. are taking up measures like Los Angeles'. The grower's biggest buyer is Wal-Mart, an inviting target for people already angry at that chain's treatment of its own workers. After the LA City Council vote, Maria Elena Durazo, at the time still the head of the county labor federation, warned Gerawan Farming of a possible boycott: "You will not be welcome in the stores of Los Angeles if that's the next thing these workers ask us to do."

Boycotts can take time to have an effect -- the original UFW grape boycott lasted five years. And once started, they're hard to stop. But targeted boycotts have been very successful in recent years at forcing garment companies selling clothes on college campuses to recognize unions in sweatshops. The Farm Labor Organizing Committee won an agreement covering thousands of North Carolina farm workers several years ago by successfully boycotting Mount Olive pickles. By taking on the largest consumers of Gerawan's Prima brand fruit, like school districts, the UFW could make a big dent in sales. Cesar Chavez believed that cutting off 5% of sales was normally enough to make a boycott successful.

The Impact of Decertification

Decertification is more than just the key to undoing the original election that required Gerawan to bargain. If holding an election can't actually lead to a contract, there's not much reason for workers anywhere to risk their jobs supporting a union. Growers far beyond Gerawan, therefore, have an interest in the outcome - the reason why the Grape and Tree Fruit League and national conservative groups are paying attention.

A stronger union in California fields could raise wages (and growers' labor costs), which are far lower now than they were thirty years ago when the UFW was at its strongest. One recent study found that tens of thousands of Mexican indigenous farm workers in California receive less than minimum wage. It is common today to find workers sleeping in cars in parking lots during the grape picking season, or even under trees and on hillsides. Outside the state wages and living conditions are often worse.

The ALRB's responsibility is to make the election and negotiation process work. This March Governor Jerry Brown appointed William Gould IV chair of the Agricultural Labor Relations Board. Gould is an African American emeritus law professor at Stanford University, and former chair of the National Labor Relations Board under President Clinton. In answering questions from the legislature, Gould expressed concern over long delays and the low number of petitions for representation. "Enforcement of collective bargaining agreements as imposed upon the parties through the Mandatory Mediation and Conciliation ... must be expedited by the Board," he urged.

In the Senate Rules Committee hearing on his nomination, he told legislators that he wanted "to make mediation and conciliation more streamlined, so parties don't wait months." In the case of labor law violations he advocated using temporary injunctions to get relief "without waiting years for them to play out."

The board's operations, however, are constrained by reduced budgets. To make the process work faster the ALRB needs more hearing officers and staff, which means Gould will have to use his political skills to convince the Governor and legislature to give it more money.

Meanwhile, enforcement of the mediator's contract at Gerawan seems far away to the company's workers. While the grower continues to operate without it, UFW supporters like Salas say they face retaliation. "I've worked for Gerawan since 1999," he told Capital and Main. "The foreman realized I was for the union when they began passing around the petition and I wouldn't sign it. " He was denied work along with his wife in their normal crew. "What the company really wants is for us to quit," he charges.

David Bacon is an author, photographer, immigrant rights activists, see links below

Notes

THE REALITY CHECK - David Bacon blog http://davidbaconrealitycheck.blogspot.com

EN LOS CAMPOS DEL NORTE: Farm worker photographs on the U.S./Mexico border wall
http://us7.campaign-archive2.com/?u=fc67a76dbb9c31aaee896aff7&id=0644c65ae5&e=dde0321ee7
Youtube interview about the show with Alfonso Caraveo (Spanish) https://www.youtube.com/watch?v=lJeE1NO4c_M&feature=youtu.be

The Real News: Does Obama's Support of TPP Contradict his Immigration Policy?

http://therealnews.com/t2/index.php?option=com_content&task=view&id=31&Itemid=74&jumival=13034

The Real News: Putting off Immigration Reform Angers Grassroots Activists
http://therealnews.com/t2/index.php?option=com_content&task=view&id=31&Itemid=74&jumival=12352

The Real News: Immigration Reform Requires Dismantling NAFTA and Respecting Migrants' Rights/ Immigrant Communities Resist Deportations
http://therealnews.com/t2/index.php?option=com_content&task=view&id=31&Itemid=74&jumival=10938
http://therealnews.com/t2/index.php?option=com_content&task=view&id=31&Itemid=74&jumival=10933

David Bacon radio review of the movie, Cesar Chavez
https://soundcloud.com/kpfa-fm-94-1-berkeley/upfronts-david-bacon-reviews-film-on-cesar-chavez-and-the-grape-strike

Interviews with David Bacon about his book, The Right to Stay Home:

Book TV: A presentation of the ideas in The Right to Stay Home at the CUNY Graduate Center
http://booktv.org/Watch/14961/The+Right+to+Stay+Home+How+US+Policy+Drives+Mexican+Migration.aspx

KPFK - Uprisings with Sonali Kohatkar
http://uprisingradio.org/home/2013/09/27/the-right-to-stay-home-how-us-policy-drives-mexican-migration/

KPFA - Upfront with Brian Edwards Tiekert
https://soundcloud.com/kpfa-fm-94-1-berkeley/david-bacon-on-upfront-9-20

Photoessay: Mexico City marches against NAFTA and to protect its oil and electricity

http://desinformemonos.org/2014/02/veinte-anos-de-tlc-veinte-anos-de-resistencia/

Resiliance Undocumented - video about day laborers on San Francisco street corners

http://healthequity.sfsu.edu/resilience-undocumented

Books by David Bacon

The Right to Stay Home: How US Policy Drives Mexican Migration (Beacon Press, 2013)
http://www.beacon.org/productdetails.cfm?PC=2328

Illegal People -- How Globalization Creates Migration and Criminalizes Immigrants (Beacon Press, 2008)
Recipient: C.L.R. James Award, best book of 2007-2008
http://www.beacon.org/Illegal-People-P780.aspx

Communities Without Borders (Cornell University/ILR Press, 2006)
http://www.cornellpress.cornell.edu/book/?GCOI=80140100558350

The Children of NAFTA, Labor Wars on the U.S./Mexico Border (University of California, 2004)
http://www.ucpress.edu/books/pages/9989.html

For more articles and images, see http://dbacon.igc.org

How Many Governments Can Boast 83% Approval Rating by Their People?

The Greek People Rise Up

By Aris Anagnos

The Greek elections of January 25, 2015 are nothing less than a peaceful revolution accomplished by free elections. The triumphant winner is the SYRIZA Party, an acronym for "Coalition of the Radical Left." This formerly small leftist party, won 36.4% of the popular vote, 8.5% more than the runner up right wing New Democracy Party, which formed the majority of the previous government.

SYRIZA is an amalgam of various leftists, Socialists, Communists and other radicals. It includes the 92 year old national hero, Manolis Glezos, who, as a young communist member of the Resistance climbed the steep rear of the Acropolis one night in 1941, during the German occupation, and brought down the German flag with the swastika, replacing it with a Greek flag. I was there when, the next morning, all of us Athenians could watch with elation and tears the Greek flag flying over the Acropolis, until the Nazis took it down. The new Prime Minister, the 40 year old Alexis Tsipras, a civil engineer and his wife, also an engineer, met first when both were members of the Young Communist League.

Under Greek law, the party with the highest vote gets a bonus of 50 votes in the 300 member unicameral Parliament. SYRIZA obtained 149 votes, and in order to secure a majority Tsipras invited a small right wing party, the Independent Greeks, to join the cabinet thus securing a parliamentary majority of 162 votes. That party had also opposed the austerity policy.

Greece had fallen into serious debt because of the heavy defense expenditures required because of threats by its aggressive neighbor, Turkey, the perennial darling of the Pentagon. Contributing to the enormous deficit were extensive tax evasions by the rich and corruption by the previous government officials who favored their pals with lucrative contracts. A former minister of Defense is in jail because he enriched himself enormously from illegal commissions obtained for military contracts he approved. He should have lots of company, but he is a rare example.

With Greece on the verge of bankruptcy, the right wing government in power addressed itself to the European Union and the International Monetary Fund for assistance. The European partners, eager to avoid the disruption which Greece`s exit from the Euro would cause, under the leadership of Germany, imposed conditions of brutal austerity which plunged the country into a deep depression. The GDP fell by more than 25%, unemployment reached 27%, salaries, wages of those still working and pensions were cut and taxes were raised. Misery and hunger were widespread. Homes and condominiums of those who could not pay the taxes were foreclosed, and the taxes were added to the electric bill as a means of collection. Those behind in their payments had their electricity cut off. New taxes on heating oil made it unaffordable and people burned wood instead, leading to a catastrophic smog in the Athens basin, which is surrounded by mountains on three sides. In addition, the cutting of firewood depleted the precious few forests near Athens. Teachers, doctors and other public servants were laid off by the tens of thousands, destroying both the educational and public medical care system of the country.

The previous government, a coalition of the conservative New Democracy and PASOK (Socialist) parties, would obediently comply with any restrictions demanded by the international lenders in order to get the next installment of financial aid. Most of that went to service previous debts and never entered the Greek economy. The government privatized publicly owned utility and other companies at give-away prices to raise revenue. Is it any wonder that SYRIZA rose to an almost revolutionary force?

The day after victory, SYRIZA announced many immediate steps to relieve the suffering. The electricity, cut off for non- payment, would be immediately restored to those residents. The foreclosures of primary residences and further privatizations would stop. A program to create 300,000 new jobs (3% of the ten million population of Greece) would be started and many other measures to relieve human suffering were started, including free food distribution to the poor. The money for all these programs would come from strict enforcement of tax collection from the tax evading rich and elimination of corruption. In addition there would be a reduction of the highest salaries to public servants in order to increase those at the lowest levels. Greece also demanded payment of a billion eight hundred million profit earned by the European Central Bank on Greek bonds.

A reduction of the foreign debt was immediately ruled out by the creditors, so the Greek Prime Minister and the Finance Minister are currently proposing to the foreign lenders a drawing out of the payments and a lowering of the interest rate, plus a six months "bridge" program of debt relief in order to start a recovery of the devastated economy. As of February 12, there was no agreement in the negotiations with the European lenders and the IMF. An agreement is hoped for at the meeting of February 15th.

Nevertheless, the energetic policies of the new Greek government have overwhelming support among the Greek people. A new poll released on February 13th by the prominent TV station ALPHA shows an approval rating of 83%, including a favorable shift of many voters who voted for other parties in the January 25 elections. How many governments in the entire world can boast of an 83% approval rating by their peoples?

Aris Anognos was born in Athens, Greece and came to the US in 1946. He has been active in human and civil rights and progressive politics. He is a past President of the ACLU of Southern California, the Americans for Democratic Action, the American Hellenic Council, and the Humanitarian Law Project.

A Sympathetic Critique of Naomi Klein's 'This Changes Everything'

By David Schwartzman

Naomi Klein's book "This Changes Everything: Capitalism Vs the Climate" (TCE) is a very welcome contribution to the climate justice movement, especially because of its powerful critique of neo-liberal capitalism with respect to its role in creating the threat of climate catastrophe and its ongoing inadequacy in confronting this challenge. Klein's description of the global climate justice movement is inspiring, especially coming from someone who has been close to Bill McKibben and 350.org.

But taking TCE as seriously as it richly deserves demands a critique which identifies its silences regarding critical aspects of this unprecedented threat to the future of human civilization and biodiversity as we know it. Here are a few reviews from the left with the last two being the most critical, but I recommend you read the book first: http://monthlyreview.org/2015/02/01/crossing-the-river-of-fire/, https://radicalantipode.files.wordpress.com/2015/01/book-review_huber-on-klein.pdf and perhaps the best, by Suren Moodliar, "System Change Without Class Struggle?, Socialism and Democracy (2015), 29 (1), 141-151. I do disagree with Suren Moodliar's argument that TCE leaves out the importance of class struggle. All the climate justice movements which are so vividly described constitute class struggle, multi-dimensional and transnational, even though the global political Subject is not yet fully conscious of itself. Only when this happens, and soon, will we have a chance to avoid climate catastrophe.

Here is my first point of critique. TCE does outline radical reforms necessary to avoid climate catastrophe, much along the lines of our strategic objective, a Green New Deal. But, it fails to name the real alternative to unsustainable capitalism, ecosocialism, the only viable socialism of the 21st Century, nor does it provide a concrete vision of the "other world that is possible" after capitalism is eliminated on our planet. Is this asking too much? Perhaps, since I do recognize there is a real possibility that Naomi

Klein is a closet (eco)socialist but is very careful to calibrate what she says, not too far ahead of popular consciousness, even within the broad climate justice movement. However, I will focus my critique on TCE's lack of analysis of a critical obstacle to implementing a prevention program to avoid climate catastrophe, the Imperial Agenda of US and transnational capital and along the way flesh out some of the essential components of a just transition from fossil fuels to a global renewable energy infrastructure.

Getting Clear on the Military

TCE is virtually silent on the role of imperialism as a critical obstacle to implementing a Prevention Program to avoid Catastrophic Climate Change (C3). This obstacle is briefly alluded to when the US military is identified as the biggest consumer of petroleum on the planet. Yet, according to the figures she cites for 2011 (p.113), the total carbon dioxide equivalent emissions of the Department of Defense is less than 0.2% of the global total for that year (data from the International Energy Agency). Yes, the US military budget is identified as a potential source of revenue for a prevention program to avoid C3, but TCE fails to confront why the Military Industrial (Fossil Fuel, Nuclear, State Terror and Surveillance) Complex ("MIC"), at the core of 21st Century Capitalism, is such a huge block to implementation of such a prevention program.

Yes, the MIC is likewise the Molochian Instrument of Carnage. In John Milton's Paradise Lost, Moloch is one of the greatest warriors of the fallen angels: "First MOLOCH, horrid King besmear'd with blood Of human sacrifice, and parents tears ".

First, the obvious. The MIC is indeed the source of colossal waste of energy and material resources which should go to meet human and nature's needs on our planet. But most relevant to the threat of C3 is the role of the Pentagon as the "global oil-protection service" (Michael Klare's description), for the MIC and its imperial agenda, indeed for the transnational capital class itself. And this agenda blocks the global cooperation and equity required for a successful prevention program for C3, while the time window of opportunity rapidly decreases.

A global wind/solar transition replacing the present unsustainable energy supplies must be parasitic on these supplies, just as the industrial fossil fuel revolution was parasitic on biomass (plant) energy, until it replaced the former supply with sufficient capacity. Liquid oil has the lowest carbon footprint of the fossil fuels (taking into account the significant leakage to the atmosphere of methane from natural gas), and is therefore the preferred energy source to make a renewable energy transition, aside from energy derived from a growing renewable infrastructure (for more on this subject go to www.solarUtopia.org). Thus, oil rich countries in the Mid-

East and South America (e.g., Venezuela) will be valuable partners in this transition by providing the needed petroleum, while using the minimum amount possible to keep carbon emissions to a minimum.

With the collaboration of Quincy Saul, I presented our paper at the Moving beyond Capitalism meeting last August in San Miguel de Allende, Mexico, with the title "An Ecosocialist Horizon for Venezuela: A Solar Communist Horizon for the World". Its main focus was how Venezuela could use its oil to bring about a solar transition in Latin America and in the world. While TCE does recognize the role of Venezuelan oil exports in sharply reducing poverty in that country, it fails to mention this immense opportunity. But what about "solar communism"? Check out my article in *Dialogue & Initiative 2014* "Solar Communism Revisited" with its reprint of my 1996 paper from *Science & Society*. And I recommend readers check out the recent interview of Quincy Saul, "On Climate Satyagraha" at http://www.counterpunch.org/2015/04/10/on-climate-satyagraha/.

To close on a positive note, we should recognize that confronting the twin threats of C3 and nuclear war is an unprecedented opportunity to end the rule of capital on our planet, precisely because the main obstacle to elimination of these threats is the MIC. Let this inspire the youth of our planet and we can be confident that another world is indeed possible in the 21st Century.

David Schwartzman is a retired professor specializing in environmental studies and an activist. He was a Green Party candidate for Green Party Shadow Senator from Washington D.C. in 2014.

Lies and Myths About Greece and Europe's Debt

By Conn Hallinan

March 15, 2015 - Myths are dangerous precisely because they rely more on cultural memory and prejudice than facts, and behind the current crisis between Greece and the European Union (EU) lays a fable that bears little relationship to why Athens and a number of other countries in the 28-member organization find themselves in deep distress.

The tale is a variation of Aesop's allegory of the industrious ant and the lazy, fun-loving grasshopper, with the "northern countries" - Germany, the Netherlands, Britain, Finland - playing the role of the ant, and Greece, Spain, Portugal, and Ireland the part of the grasshopper.

The ants are sober and virtuous - led by the frugal Swabian housefrau, German Chancellor Angela Merkel - the grasshoppers are spendthrift, corrupt lay-abouts who have spent themselves into trouble and now must pay the piper.

The problem is that this myth bears almost no relationship to the actual roots of the crisis or what the solutions might be. And it perpetuates a fable that the debt is the fault of individual countries rather than a serious crisis at the very heart of the EU.

First, a Little Myth Busting

The European debt crisis goes back to the end of the roaring '90s when the banks were flush with money and looking for ways to raise their bottom lines. One major strategy was to pour money into real estate, which had the effect of creating bubbles, particularly in Spain and Ireland. In the latter, from 1999 to 2007, bank loans for Irish real estate jumped 1,730 percent, from 5 million Euros to 96.2 million Euros, or more than half the GDP of the Irish Republic. Housing prices increased 500 percent. "It was not the public sector but the private sector that went haywire in Ireland," concludes Financial Times analyst Martin Wolf.

Spain, which had a budget surplus and a low debt ratio, went through much the same process, and saw an identical jump in housing prices: 500 percent.

In both countries there was corruption, but it wasn't the penny ante variety of tax evasion or profit skimming. Politicians - eager for a piece of the action and generous "donations" - waived zoning rules and environmental regulations, and cut sweetheart tax deals. Hundreds of thousands of housing projects went up, many of them never to be occupied.

The Bankster Trick

Then the American banking crisis hit in 2008, and the bottom fell out. Suddenly, the ants were in trouble. But not really, because the ants have a trick: they gamble and the grasshoppers pay.

The "trick," as Joseph Stiglitz, Nobel Laureate in economics, points out, is that Europe (and the U.S.) have moved those debts "from the private sector to the public sector - a well-established pattern over the past half-century."

Fintan O'Toole, author of "Ship of Fools: How Stupidity and Corruption Sank the Celtic Tiger," estimates that to save the Irish-Anglo Bank, Irish taxpayers shelled out 30 billion Euros, a sum that was the equivalent of the island's entire tax revenues for 2009. The European Central Bank - which, along with the International Monetary Fund (IMF) and the European Commission, make up the "Troika" - strong-armed Ireland into adopting austerity measures that tanked the country's economy, doubled the unemployment rate, increased consumer taxes, and forced many of the country's young people to emigrate. Almost half of Ireland's income tax now goes just to service the interest on its debts.

Poor Portugal. It had a solid economy and a low debt ratio, but currency speculators drove up interest rates on borrowing beyond what the government could afford, and the European Central Bank refused to intervene. The result was that Lisbon was forced to swallow a "bailout" that was laden with austerity measures that, in turn, torpedoed its economy.

In Greece's case corruption was at the heart of the crisis, but not the popular version about armies of public workers and tax dodging oligarchs. There are rich tax dodgers aplenty in Greece, but Germany, Sweden, and many other European countries spend more of their GDP on services than does Athens. Greece spends 44.6 percent of its GDP on its citizens, less than the EU average and below Germany's 46 percent and Sweden's 55 percent.

And as for being lazy: The Greeks work 600 hours more a year than Germans.

According to economist Mark Blyth, author of "Austerity: The History of a Dangerous Idea," Greek public spending through the 2000s is "really on track and quite average in comparison to everyone else's," and the so-called flood of "public sector jobs" consisted of "14,000 over two years." All the talk of the profligate Greek government is "a lot of nonsense" and just "political cover for the fact that what we've done is bail out some of the richest people in European society and put the cost on some of the poorest."

There was a "score" in Greece. However, it had nothing to do with free spending, but was a scheme dreamed up by Greek politicians, bankers, and the American finance corporation, Goldman Sachs.

Greece's application for EU membership in 1999 was rejected because its budget deficit in relation to its GDP was over 3 percent, the cutoff line for joining. That's where Goldman Sachs came in. For a fee rumored to be $200 million (some say three times that), the multinational giant essentially cooked the books to make Greece look like it cleared the bar. Then Greece's political and economic establishment hid the scheme until the 2008 crash shattered the illusion.

It was the busy little ants, not the fiddling grasshoppers that brought on the European debt crisis.

American, German, French, and Dutch banks had to know that they were creating an unstable real estate bubble - a 500 percent jump in housing prices is the very definition of the beast - but kept right on lending because they were making out like bandits.

When the bubble popped and Europe went into recession, Greece was forced to apply for a "bailout" from the Troika. In exchange for 172 billion Euros, the Greek government instituted an austerity program that saw economic activity decline 25 percent, and unemployment rise to 27 percent (and over 50 percent for young Greeks). The cutbacks slashed pensions, wages, and social services, and drove 44 percent of the population into poverty.

Virtually all of the "bailout" - 89 percent - went to the banks that gambled in the 1999 to 2007 real estate casino. What the Greek - as well as Spaniards, Portuguese, and Irish - got was misery.

There are other EU countries, including Italy and France that, while not in quite the same boat as the "distressed four," are under pressure to bring down their debt ratios.

But what are those debts?

This past summer, the Committee for a Citizen's Audit on the Public Debt issued a report on France, a country that is currently instituting austerity measures to bring its debt in line with the magic "three percent" ratio. What the committee concluded was that 60 percent of the French public debt was "illegitimate."

More than 18 other countries, including Brazil, Portugal, Ecuador, Greece and Spain, have done the same "audit," and, in each case, found that increased public spending was not the cause of deficits. From 1978 to 2012, French public spending actually declined by two GDP points.

The main culprit in the debt crisis was a fall in tax revenues resulting from massive tax cuts for corporations and the wealthy. According to Razmig Keucheyan, sociologist and author of "The Left Hemisphere," this "neoliberal mantra" that was supposed to increase investment and employment did the opposite.

According to the study, the second major reason was the increase in interest rates that benefits creditors and speculators. Had interest rates remained stable during the 1990s, debt would be significantly lower.

Keucheyan argues that tax reductions and interest rates are "political decisions" and that "public deficits do not grow naturally out of the normal course of social life. They are deliberately inflicted on society by the dominant classes to legitimize austerity policies that will allow the transfer of value from the working classes to the wealthy ones."

The International Labor Organization recently found that wages have, indeed, stalled or declined throughout the EU over the past decade.

The audit movement calls for repudiating debt that results from "the service of private interests" as opposed to the "wellbeing of the people." In 2008, Ecuador canceled 70 percent of its debt as "illegitimate."

How this plays out in the current Greek-EU crisis is not clear. The Syriza government is not asking to cancel the debt - though it would certainly like a write-down - but only that it be given time to let the economy grow. The recent four-month deal may give Athens some breathing room, but the ants are still demanding austerity and tensions are high.

What seems clear is that Germany and its allies are trying to force Syriza into accepting conditions that will undermine its support in Greece and demoralize anti-austerity movements in other countries.

The U.S. can play a role in this - President Obama has already called for easing the austerity policies - through its domination of the IMF. By itself Washington can outvote Germany, the Netherlands, and Finland, and could exert pressure on the two other Troika members to compromise. Will it? Hard to say, but the Americans are certainly a lot more nervous about Greece exiting the Eurozone than Germany.

But the key to a solution is exploding the myth.

That has already begun. Over the past few weeks, demonstrators in Greece, Spain, Italy, Germany, Portugal, Great Britain, Belgium and Austria have poured into the streets to support Syriza's stand against the Troika. "The Left has to work together having as its common goal the elimination of predatory capitalism," says Maite Mola, vice-president of the European Left organization and member of the Portuguese parliament. "And the solution should be European."

In the end, the grasshoppers might just turn Aesop's fable upside down.

This article originally appeared at Conn Hallinan's blog, Dispatches From the Edge.

PDA, the Congressional Progressive Caucus and the People's Budget

By Randy Shannon

The Congressional Progressive Caucus (CPC) is the center of gravity of left and progressive politics in the United States today. Over the past two decades it has grown steadily in size, sophistication, and impact. Today its membership listed on the CPC website consists of 68 Representatives and one Senator.

The members of the CPC are sent to Congress by the majority of the 37.5 million people of voting age in their districts. The CPC represents a total population of 48.5 million of which 57.6% are white, 21.2% are African American, 23.7% are Latino, and 8.4% are Asian. The population is 48.7% male and 51.3% female. The population base of the CPC includes 18.4% of people living below the poverty level and 15.8% without health insurance.

In addition to their support among the majority of voters, CPC members enjoy the financial and political support of various labor organizations, human rights organizations, and left and progressive political organizations. These groups assist the CPC in crafting its political and legislative strategy and work to build grassroots support to achieve its goals.

The goals of the CPC are framed by its core principles.

- Fighting for economic justice and security for all.
- Protecting and preserving our civil rights and civil liberties.
- Promoting global peace and security.
- Advancing environmental protections and energy independence.

In his 2008 campaign Vice President Joe Biden said: "Don't tell me what you value, show me your budget, and I'll tell you what you value." The Congressional Progressive Caucus has introduced its own People's Budget proposal to Congress year after year. The People's Budget represents the practical democratic agenda of the US progressive majority and speaks

CONGRESSIONAL PROGRESSIVE CAUCUS
THE PEOPLE'S BUDGET
A RAISE FOR AMERICA

The People's Budget: A Raise for America

8.4 million good-paying jobs by 2018
$1.9 trillion investment in America's future
$820 billion infrastructure and transportation improvements

directly to the expectations of its members' electorate. On March 24, 2015 the People's Budget garnered 96 votes, 22% of House members, and a majority of Democrats for the first time in five years.

The Role of PDA

At a Progressive Democrats of America roundtable, Rev. Lennox Yearwood, a PDA Board Member and leader of the Hip Hop Caucus, coined an apt slogan: "Demonstration without Legislation Equals Frustration." This idea reflects the role of PDA, a grassroots organization that supports the People's Budget and works to nominate progressive candidates in Democratic primaries and to support incumbent CPC members. PDA's inside/outside strategy is designed to build a progressive bloc tied to the people's movements within the Democratic Party structure.

PDA chapters across the country promoted the People's Budget among political actors and in the people's movement. PDA provides a monthly platform for members of Congress and movement leaders to discuss current issues and legislation with the live-streamed Progressive Roundtable from Washington. PDA members also engage in a monthly lobby effort, visiting between 350 and 450 local Congressional offices each month. The local office visits are followed by visits in DC and phone calls to key members around high priority issues of the month. PDA has led the way in campaigning for passage of the ERA in several states and for an ERA extension bill in Congress. PDA also continues to play a key organizing role in the fight against the Trans Pacific Partnership and Fast Track authorization.

The People's Budget attacks income inequality, student debt, climate change, joblessness, the deficit, and the crumbling infrastructure. It opens the way to single payer healthcare, cuts the military budget, provides for affordable housing, and establishes public financing of election campaigns.

The People's Budget represents the highest level of organization of the progressive majority on the political level. It provides a framework for broad unity and a program around which a majority can organize to defeat the hegemony of finance capital and its program of war and austerity. The People's Budget is a necessary stage and the immediate goal for the establishment of true democracy in the USA, a prerequisite for achieving a more advanced society.

The People's Budget fixes an economy that, for too long, has failed to provide the opportunities American families need to get ahead. Despite their skills and work ethic, most American workers and families are so financially strapped from increasing income inequality that their paychecks barely cover basic necessities. They earn less and less as corporations and the wealthy continue amassing record profits. It has become clear to American workers that the system is rigged.

The People's Budget levels the playing field and creates economic opportunity by increasing the pay of middle- and low-income Americans. More customers and higher consumer spending advance American businesses, not tax cuts and relaxed regulations. The People's Budget drives a full economic recovery by creating high-quality jobs and reducing family expenses, restoring the buying power of working Americans.

The People's Budget closes tax loopholes that companies use to ship jobs overseas. It creates fair tax rates for millionaires and provides needed relief to low- and middle-income families. It invests in debt-free college, workforce training and small businesses within our communities, helping return our economy to full employment and giving a raise to Americans who need it most. Investments in The People's Budget boost employment and wages by addressing some of the biggest challenges of our time: repairing America's rapidly aging roads and bridges, upgrading our energy systems to address climate change, keeping our communities safe, and preparing our young people to thrive as citizens and workers.

A fair wage is more than the size of a paycheck. It's having enough hours, paid overtime, sick and parental leave, and affordable health and childcare. It's being able to afford a good education for your kids and never living in fear that your job will be sent overseas. It is knowing that you can make ends meet at the end of the month. The People's Budget helps achieve that with a raise for American workers, a raise for struggling families and a boost to America's long-term global competitiveness.

A RAISE FOR AMERICA
- Creates more than 8 million good jobs by 2018.
- Increases functionality of Worker Protection Agencies.
- Includes a four percent raise for federal workers.
- Provides Paid Leave Initiative and Child Care.
- Supports a minimum wage increase and Collective Bargaining.

AUSTERITY TO PROSPERITY
- Repeals sequester and all Budget Control Act spending caps.
- Increases discretionary funding to invest in working families.
- Reverses harmful cuts and enhances social safety net.
- Invests in veterans, women, communities of color and their families.

FAIR INDIVIDUAL TAXES
- Equalizes tax rates for investment income and income from work.
- Returns to Clinton-era tax rates for households making over $250,000 and implements new brackets for those making over $1 million.
- Expands the Earned Income Tax Credit and the Child Care Credit.

FAIR CORPORATE TAXES
- Eliminates the ability of US corporations to defer taxes on offshore profits.
- Ends corporate inversions that allow US companies to merge offshore to avoid taxes.
- Enacts a Financial Transaction Tax on various financial market transactions.
- Ends unlimited executive pay tax write-offs.

EDUCATIONAL OPPORTUNITIES FOR EVERY STUDENT
- Provides debt-free college to every student.
- Allows refinancing of student loans.
- Invests in K-12 and provides free pre-school.

AFFORDABLE HEALTH CARE
- Repeals excise tax on high-priced workers plans and replaces with public option.
- Implements drug price negotiation for Medicare.
- Reauthorizes Children's Health Insurance Program.
- Allows states to transition to single-payer health care systems.

PROTECTING OUR ENVIRONMENT
· Closes tax loopholes and ends subsidies provided to oil, gas and coal companies.
· Enacts a price on carbon pollution without hurting low-income families.
· Invests in clean and renewable energy and green manufacturing.

SUSTAINABLE DEFENSE
· Modernizes our defense posture to create sustainable baseline defense spending.
· Ends emergency funding for Overseas Contingency Operations.
· Increases funding for diplomacy and invests in job transition programs.

COMPREHENSIVE IMMIGRATION REFORM
· Implements comprehensive immigration reform, including a pathway to citizenship.

ACCESS TO HOUSING
· Fully funds programs to make housing affordable and accessible for all Americans.

PUBLIC FINANCING OF CAMPAIGNS
· Funds public financing of campaigns to curb special interest influence in politics.

Randy Shannon is a PDA Pennsylvania Organizer and PDA Economic & Social Justice Team Coordinator

American Sniper, Why So Popular?

By Lila Garrett

Never see a horror film just before you go to sleep. I'm talking about American Sniper, and for people who define war as a capital crime that's what it was....a horror film. Mass murder presented as heroism.

Navy Seal, Chris Kyle who killed 160 Iraqis of all ages...children, grandparents, whoever appeared within range....is presented as a great American hero. His passive-aggressive insanity is portrayed by Bradley Cooper as "depth, inner conflict, a passion for his country." And since Cooper is a good actor, and a great kisser, it makes you want to make-out with him instead of what you should be doing.....running a mile in the opposite direction.

Not only is this NOT an anti-war picture, it makes anyone who doesn't own an AK .338 Lapua Magnum-chambered McMillan TAC-338 sniper rifle, feel like a sissy. This is one dangerous film. But what do we expect from Clint Eastwood, master of nastiness? He's a right wing zealot who happens to know how to put together a film and make it look even-handed. A little something for everybody sells tickets, and you just have to look at the response to American Sniper to know how expert he is at that. If he'd just stick to talking to empty chairs we'd all be better off. At the end Kyle is killed by a "deranged" veteran, and not a moment too soon.

A word of advice: don't see it.

The mystery is, why is it #1 at the box office. What is it about unbridled anger that so attracts Americans? Is it a sign of our own frustration which we are unable to articulate? Who are we really angry at? Is it the people we elect to represent us who instead represent the rich and powerful?

When you remember actively campaigning for candidates who share your convictions, when you believed their promises ..... and then they're elected and you never hear about that agenda again, does it gall you?

You spend years watching them roll over, kissing up to the other side, withdrawing the social safety net that our taxes pay for, increasing the defense budget so you can enable the Chris Kyles of the world to kill harder and faster, developing drones to make killing more efficient and widespread. And with masses of drones and hundreds of bombing missions a week, we're reaching the point where a single sniper will become nostalgia. That sniper's photo will end up in a drawer next to Grandma's cameo. We'll soon be saying ah the good old days when we did our killing by hand. It was so much neater then.

Interesting how easily the United States bounces from war to war, keeping the number of casualties unreported. Those casualties are now apparently regarded as top secret.

Are our journalists forbidden from reporting them? Are they even allowed on the ground? The silence on the extent of the dead and wounded is deafening. Recently we've heard the number 6,000 in collateral damage. But that number came and went....fast...without any details.

In his State of the Union address our President certainly didn't mention that. And while he bragged about the improving economy, he didn't mention where all the new jobs are coming from? The defense buildup perhaps? The tremendous growth spurt of drones in our country? Here we are dropping these little electronic killers with awesome regularity on Iraq, Syria, Somalia, Pakistan, Yemen, Afghanistan...wherever the spirit moves us... and not one word was said in his once a year major speech to the nation. Instead he filled it with his new bag of goodies: free community colleges, raising the minimum wage, saving Social Security and Medicare, giving immigrants a fair shake, creating a Washington that gets out of the people's way instead of blocking them. All worthy goals.

Yes, the first half of his speech was the feel good hour. Interesting to watch John Boehner, who for some strange reason is permitted to sit behind the President during his star moment. Like a Greek chorus, he and the Vice President commented with smirks and/or smiles on every word being said.

For Boehner the first half of the speech was the all smirk section. That was the Roosevelt-esque social programs half. But he got to his feet and applauded when the President talked about fighting Isis. He got up even faster and applauded again when Obama made a pitch for upping the ante in the war.

Apparently they both still think we can kill our way out of the world's rise of terrorist gangs. No matter that the more troops and hardware we send in, the more these rebel bands multiply. Richard Engel NBC/MSNBC war correspondent based in Turkey, said we have been killing a thousand members of Isis a month. But they are constantly replaced by 1500.

The more bombing and drone missions we send into Syria and Iraq, the more young people flood into these rebel groups. They have nothing to lose including their own lives, which they feel they'll lose anyway if they don't fight back. Like Chris Kyle, all they can see is a world that is hostile to them...and they are not going to let that world win.

John Boehner looked worried during Obama's speech. He wants to rev up our military action against Iran and obviously he wasn't satisfied by the Republican response given by Joni Ernst, the simple minded Senator from Iowa.

So now, unilaterally, Boehner has invited Netanyahu in February to speak before the Congress in exactly the same star spot as our peerless leader. What is he thinking? That Netanyahu should fill Obama's shoes as our leader? How crazy can it get? How lawless? Since when does a foreign leader come in to replace our democratically elected President. Warts and all...we did elect him. Twice as he pointed out. So what is going on here?

And if we can't kill our way out of the growth of these terrorist groups, how do we get rid of them?

Would that Chris Kyle were still around to advise us.

Since he's not, let's settle for Dennis Kucinch. Luckily he's with us now.......

Lila Garrett is the host of "Connect the Dots" which airs on KPFK, Pacific radio in Los Angeles, CA.

Is the United States Inching Towards Fascism?

By Mark Solomon

Is the United Inching towards Fascism? Yes and No.

That is not a dodge or an effort to be coy. The answer to the question is rooted in the ebb and flow of political engagement as the sources of the fascist threat are recognized and contested. It is rooted in the capacity of masses to fight for the preservation of democracy and to defeat the right wing that is the purveyor of fascism.

Thus, fascism and the battle against it cannot be separated from the interpenetration of material circumstances and political struggle. The outcome of that struggle will determine the victory or defeat of the fascist danger. Further, the outcome cannot be predicted with certainty. It will depend on the rising consciousness and activity of masses that connect the deteriorating conditions of their lives with the threat of fascism.

There exists a broad front of extreme reaction ranging from secret paramilitary units such as the violently racist "League of the South," the Aryan Nation and armed vigilantes at the country's southern borders. There are assorted white supremacist, neo-Nazi and anti-Semitic organizations, some functioning under a banner of Christian fundamentalism. There are "respectable" organizations such as the Tea Party that mask extreme right wing objectives under attacks on "big government" and "liberal elites." There is a gaggle of right wing reactionaries in Congress whose agenda abets fascist objectives. There are ultra-reactionary voices in media (shock radio and inflammatory Internet sites) that spew hatred for women, gay, lesbian and transgender people and oppressed nationalities. To the extent that the Fox media empire practices vile class warfare upon the poor, working class movements and communities of color, it can be classified as a vessel of incipient fascism.

Those formations constitute a nurturing ground for fascism. They are ultra-nationalist, white supremacist, intensely anti-immigrant, homophobic, and supportive of police-inflicted violence upon people of color, hostile to women and women's reproductive choice, strongly threatening to free speech and democratic rights in general.

There exists a neo-Nazi pseudo-cultural current, generally unknown to progressives. The Southern Poverty Law Center has identified fifty-four neo-Nazi rock bands whose music is sold online. Groups such as "White Knuckle Driver," "Skullhead," "Brutal Attack," "Kill, Baby, Kill," "White American Youth," "Prussian Blue" and others peddle songs whose titles signal the extent of their racist and anti-Semitic depravity: "Fire up the Ovens," "White Pride," "Six Million More," etc.

That current reflects pathology largely nurtured in social isolation and fear of plunging to the bottom of the social ladder. It also responds to collapsing arenas for growth and advancement under an increasingly stagnant capitalism. Its ensuing outrage is channeled away from the social system to hatred for an African American President, hatred for immigrants and hatred for all oppressed nationalities.

The 'Respectable' Far Right

The more "genteel" sector of the far right personified by the Tea Party mobilizes a large social base. It rails against "big government" and even at times against the depredations of Wall Street portraying itself as stoutly "conservative" and within the political mainstream. The Tea Party and similar currents have attracted some adherents angered by the dissolving "American Dream" of upward mobility and failing financial security.

In considering the demagogic elements of the far right, the words of Georgi Dimitroff, the leading voice of anti-fascism in the 1930s are worth recalling: "Fascism aims at the most unbridled exploitation of the masses, but it approaches them with the most artful anti-capitalist demagogy, taking advantage of the deep hatred of the working people against the plundering bourgeoisie..."

The far right's unswerving attacks on "big government" and occasionally on high finance have nothing to do with government's repressive and anti-democratic elements but are a full-bore assault on the social safety net originally built by the New Deal. Its objective is to destroy modest programs to assist the poor and efforts to partially redress social injustices. It coalesces elements calling for massive tax cuts and the end of social programs with right wing religious forces waging a war on reproductive choice and gender equality. While some components of the Tea Party far right support cuts in military spending, dominating the coalition are hawks who support a growing military and armed intervention over diplomacy.

All those complex currents constitute a dangerous and potentially lethal mass base for US fascism. But those elements ranging from armed militias to congressional reactionaries are not the crucial driving force for imposing fascist rule on the country.

The Crucial Driving Force of Fascism

There is a trend on the left that views fascism as an ideology rooted in mass pathological alienation and hatred grounded in feared loss of status. That concept stresses secondary psychological factors and fails to locate the most crucial levers of fascism in social class – in the requirements of the most reactionary elements of the ruling class to completely take over the state as an instrument of social oppression. Dimitroff's classic definition of fascism still fully characterizes the social, political and ideological content of fascism: "the open terrorist dictatorship of the most reactionary, most chauvinist and most imperialist elements of finance capital."

The experience of the Great Depression is instructive. Mass fascist movements in the 1930s arose in the midst of a collapsing economy. Organizations led by Gerald L.K. Smith, Father Charles Coughlin, William Dudley Pelley and others attracted substantial followings while spreading their anti-Semitic and racist bile. But they ultimately faded away. They were undermined by the growing power of the working class and its allies that pressured the Roosevelt administration to reject and isolate the most reactionary segments (FDR labeled them the "economic royalists") of capital. In turn, those echelons were compelled to grudgingly capitulate to the demands of the New Deal, diminishing potential support for fascist movements. At the same time, outwardly pro-fascist capital was weakened and increasingly unable to sustain support for Smith, Coughlin and the others. The final, decisive blow against 1930s fascism came with the emergence of the grand allied coalition to defeat the fascists and Nazis in World War II.

Where does the fascist threat lie today?

The greatest danger of fascism today lies within the emergence of an extremely reactionary wing of capital that promotes a "neoliberal" agenda with an attendant imposition of austerity and growing inequality.

Neoliberalism, an unrestrained exercise of state power to aggrandize capital is a byproduct of de-industrialization, globalization and the growing dominance of financial sector of the capitalist system. Banks and financial institutions rake in tens of billions in credit card debt and sub-prime mortgages (the principal generator of the economic crisis of 2008) while massive feeding of the military-industrial complex, looting and denuding industries, corporate mergers and high stakes global speculation in derivatives and credit default swaps heighten the gap between wealth and poverty.

Under the neoliberal regime, communities of color, youth, women, underpaid and unemployed workers are preyed upon in a society that is increasingly stripped of the principle of joint social responsibility for public welfare. The drive for corporate super profits in a stagnating economy promotes a growing gap between rich and poor that in turn builds the compulsion for governmental repression of increasingly restive publics stripped of resources and dignity.

Growing far right influence, operating largely though a partial takeover of the Republican Party, advances shock-and-awe austerity measures; tax cuts that serve the rich and powerful while destroying programs that help the elderly and sick; attacks on women's reproductive rights, attempts to suppress voting and to rig the electoral college; full-fledged assaults on the environmental movement; militarization of police; the destruction of public education; ongoing attacks on labor unions and on societal support for universal medical care. That is the outcome of efforts to take over the state to protect and advance concentrated wealth and to make government a prime instrument of social control and oppression.

That is well known to African Americans, Latinos, and other oppressed nationalities. The reality of repression is deeply etched in the experience of the black community of Baltimore where recently protests against yet another police murder of an African American brought large numbers of police and military to the neighborhood. That prompted a piercing observation that encapsulated the fascist threat: "The only government we see in our community is the police."

Naming Names: The Most Powerful Sources of the Fascist Danger

The strands of incipient fascism are manifested at this moment in the emergence of a super-wealthy segment of capital personified by energy-based billionaires Charles and David Koch, the Walton family that owns multibillion dollar Wal-Mart, casino magnate Sheldon Adelson and scores of others of similar ilk. Their fortunes are utilized to fully corrupt the electoral process, to buy politicians, to suppress the votes of oppressed minorities whose numbers are growing and to trash democratic choice. The American Legislative Exchange Council (ALEC) under corporate sponsorship has become a major instrument in fashioning model legislation to cripple labor, lock the working poor into low wages and rotten conditions, undermine reproductive choice and scuttle democracy in state after state.

While the repressive national security state and the massive spying apparatus of the National Security Agency (NSA) are broadly supported by corporate and government elements of both parties in promoting "the war on terror," the far right continues to be a reliable backbone for sheltering of the military-industrial complex and a 3 trillion dollar war machine. It is a crucial factor in supporting and abetting the massive spying on the public by the National Security Administration (NSA) that acts to curb and intimidate dissent.

With all that, the doors of democratic resistance and struggle have not closed. Every effort to resist austerity, inequality and anti-democratic measures contributes to the fight against incipient fascism. It is vital to understand the connections between austerity policies, growing inequality and the threat of fascism. Those links are understood by right wing capital and its political abettors that seek to suppress democracy in order to protect and advance their assault upon living standards and rights of the vast majority.

The Sources of Resistance to Fascism

Thus, resistance to fascism comes in many forms:

Resistance is inherent in the Moral Monday movement that builds a broad coalition of diverse forces to fight right wing reaction on a variety of fronts.

Resistance is advanced in the struggles of women and their allies to defend reproductive choice and advance gender equality.

Resistance is manifested in the movement for ecological survival.

Resistance is inherent in the LGBT movement and in the battle for marriage equality.

Resistance is expressed in the burgeoning movement for a living wage.

Resistance is expressed in organization of big box and fast food workers.

Resistance is manifested in a renewed fighting spirit of labor reaching out to new working class constituencies.

Resistance is expressed in the "Black Lives Matter" movement and in the growing struggles against police brutality, against mass incarceration and against the death penalty.

Resistance is embodied in the movement to amend the Constitution to nullify the Supreme Court's anti-democratic Citizens United decision.

Resistance is manifested in the mass movement for immigrant rights.

Resistance is inherent in the movement to put an end to endless wars and to ban nuclear weapons and all weapons of mass destruction.

Resistance is embodied in support for Palestine and in support for all under the yoke of oppression from Ferguson to Ramallah and beyond.

Resistance is represented in the fight for net neutrality and for democratic access to media.

Resistance is inherent in the struggle for universal single payer health care.

Resistance is expressed in the fight to defeat the anti-democratic Trans Pacific Partnership.

Resistance is inherent in the growing political struggle against austerity and inequality.

Resistance, above all, is expressed in growing alliances among diverse movements embracing the concerns rooted in class, race and gender.

As long as the struggle for democracy goes on in its many forms the right wing and the fascists can, and will, be defeated.

Mark Solomon is a retired professor of history and former co-chair of CCDS. This article was adapted from a February 7, 2015 talk for the Deerfield Progressive Forum, Deerfield Beach, Florida.

Part Three: The Struggle for 21st Century Socialism

Eleven Talking Points on 21st Century Socialism

By Carl Davidson

The recent discussions around socialism in left and progressive circles in the U.S. needs to be placed in a more substantive arena. This is an effort to do so. I take note in advance of the criticism that the following eleven working hypotheses are rather dry and formal.

But in light of the faux 'socialisms' bandied about in the headlines and sound bytes of the mass media in the wake of the financial crisis, especially the absurd claim in the media of rightwing populism that the Obama administration is Marxist and socialist, I felt something a little more rigorous might be helpful. Obviously, criticism and commentary is invited. This text, with images, is available as a slide show in the 'Study Guides' section of the Online University of the Left, at http://ouleft.org

1. Socialism's fundamental building blocks are already present in US society. The means of production, for the most part, are fully developed and in fact are stagnating under the political domination of finance capital. The US labor force, again for the most part, is highly skilled at all levels of production, management, marketing, and finance. The kernels of socialist organization are also scattered across the landscape in cooperatives, socially organized human services, and centralized and widespread mass means of many-to-many communication and supply/demand data management. Many earlier attempts at socialism did not have these advantages.

2. Socialism is first of all a democratic political system where the interests and organizations of the working class and its allies have attained and hold the preponderance of political power and thus play **the critical leading role in society.** It is still a class society, but one in a protracted transition, over hundreds of years, to a future classless society where exploiting class privileges are abolished and classes and class distinctions generally wither away, both nationally and globally. So socialism will have classes for some time, including some capitalists, because it will be a mixed economy, with both public and private ownership, even as the balance shifts over time. Family farmers and small proprietors will both exist and flourish alongside cooperatives. Innovative 'high road' entrepreneurial privately-held firms will compete with publically-owned firms, and encouraged to create new wealth within an environmentally regulated and progressively taxed system. Past efforts to build socialism have suffered from aggravated conflict between and among popular classes and lack of emphasis on building wide unity among the people.

3. Socialism at the base is a transitional economic system anchored in the social mode of production brought into being by capitalist development over several centuries. Its economic system is necessarily mixed, and makes use of markets, especially in goods and services, which are regulated, especially regarding the environment. But capital markets and wage-labor markets can be sharply restricted and even abolished in due time. Markets are a function of scarcity, and all economies of any scale in a time of scarcity have them, even if they are disguised as 'black' or 'tiered' markets. In addition to regulated markets, socialism will also feature planning, especially on the macro level of infrastructure development, in investment of public assets and funds, and other arenas where markets have failed. Planning will especially be required to face the challenges of uneven development and harsh inequalities on a global scale, as well as the challenge of moving from a carbon and uranium based energy system to one based on renewable green energy sources. The socialisms of the last century fell or stagnated due to failure to develop the proper interplay between plans and markets.

4. Socialism will be anchored in public and worker ownership of the main productive forces and natural resources. This can be achieved by various means: a) buying out major failing corporations at penny stock status, then leasing them back to the unions and having the workers in each firm-one worker, one vote-run them, b) workers directly taking ownership and control over failed and abandoned factories, c) eminent domain seizures of resources and factories, with compensation, otherwise required for the public good, and d) public funding for startups of worker-owned cooperative businesses. Socialism will also require public ownership of most finance capital institutions, including bringing the Federal Reserve under the Treasury Department and federal ownership. Lease payments from publically owned firms will go into a public investment fund, which will in turn lend money to community and worker owned banks and credit unions. A stock market will still exist for remaining publically traded firms and investments abroad, but will be strictly controlled. A stock transfer tax will be implemented. Gambling in derivatives will be outlawed. Fair trade agreements with other countries will be on a bilateral basis for mutual benefit.

5. Socialism will require democracy in the workplace of public firms and encourage it in all places of work. Workers have the right to independent unions to protect their social and daily interests, in addition to their rights as worker-owners in the governance of their firms. In addition to direct democracy at the plant level, the organizations of the working class also participate in the wider public planning process and thus democratically shape the direction of ongoing development on the macro level as well. Under socialism the government will also serve as the employer-of-last-resort. Minimum living-wage jobs will be provided for all who want to work. Socialism is committed to genuine full employment. Every citizen will have a genuine right to work.

6. Socialism will largely be gained by the working class and it allies winning the battle for democracy in politics and civil society at large, especially taking down the structures and backward laws of class, gender and racial privilege. Women have equal rights with men, and minority nationalities have equal rights with the majority. It also defends equal rights and self-determination among all nations across the globe; no nation can itself be fully free when it oppresses another. Socialism will encourage public citizenship and mass participation at every level, with open information systems, public education and transparency in its procedures. It will need a true multiparty system, with fusion voting, proportional representation and instant runoff. Given the size and diversity of our country, it is highly unlikely that any single party could adequately represent all popular interests; working class and progressive organizations will need to form common fronts. All trends are guaranteed the right to speak, organize, petition and stand for election. With public financing as an option, socialism can restrict the role of wealth in elections, moving away from a system, in effect, of "one dollar, one vote" and toward a system more reflective of "one person, one vote." These are the structural measures that can allow the majority of the people, especially the working class and its allies, to secure the political leadership of government and instruments of the state by democratic means, unless these are sabotaged by reaction. Some socialisms of the past used only limited formal democracy or simply used administrative means to implement goals, with the failure of both the goals and the overall projects. Americans are not likely to be interested in systems with elections where only one party runs and no one can lose.

7. Socialism will be a state power, specifically a democratic political order with a representative government. But the government and state components of the current order, corrupted with the thousand threads connecting it to old ruling class, will have to be broken up and replaced with new ones that are transparent, honest and serve the majority of the people. The US Constitution and Bill of Rights can still be the initial basic organizing principle for a socialist government and state. The democratic rights it has gained over the years will be protected and enhanced. Government will also be needed to organize and finance the social development benefitting the people and the environment already mentioned; but the state power behind the law will be required to compel the honest use of resources and to protect people from criminal elements, individual and organized. Forces who try to overturn and reverse the new socialist government illegally and in violation of the Constitution will not be able to do so; they will be broken up and brought to justice. Our society will need a state power for some time to come, even as its form changes. Still, government power has limits; under socialism sovereignty resides in the people themselves, and the powers of any government are necessarily restricted and subordinate to the universal and natural rights of all humankind. Attempts to ignore or reject these principles have severely harmed socialist governments and movements in the past.

8. Socialism will be a society in harmony with the natural environment, understanding that all economies are subsets of the eco-system and ignore it at their peril. In its economics, there are no such things as "externalities" to be pushed off downstream or to future generations. The nature of pending planetary disasters necessitates a high level of planning. We need to redesign communities, promote healthier foods, and rebuild sustainable agriculture—all on a global scale with high design, but on a human scale with mass participation of communities in diverse localities. Socialism will treasure and preserve the diversity of nature's bounty and end the practice of genetic modification to control the human food supply. We need growth, but intelligent growth in quality and wider knowledge with a lighter environmental footprint. A socialism that simply reproduces the wasteful expansion of an earlier capitalism creates more problems than it solves.

9. Socialism values equality, and will be a society of far greater equality of opportunity, and far less economic inequality. In addition to equal rights before the law, all citizens and residents will have equitable access to a "universal toolbox" of paid-up free public education for all who want to learn, for as far as they want and are able to go; universal public preschool care; a minimum income, as a social wage, for all who create value, whether in a workplace or otherwise; our notions of socially useful work, activity that creates value, has to be expanded beyond market definitions. Parents raising children, students learning skills, elders educating and passing traditions to younger generations--all these create value that society can in turn reward. Universal single-payer health care with retirement benefits at the level of a living wage is critical to start. Since everyone has access to employment, the existing welfare system can be abolished; individuals will be free to choose the career path and level of income targets they desire, or not. There are no handouts for those able to work, but there are also no irrational barriers to achievement.

10. Socialism is a society where religion can be freely practiced, or not, and no religion is given any special advantages over any other. Religious freedom remains a fundamental tenant of socialism, but naturally neither its practitioners nor anyone else can deny anyone the benefits and protection of civil and criminal law, especially to women and children.

11. Socialism will require an institution of armed forces. Their mission will be to defend the people and secure their interests against any enemies and help in times of natural disasters. It will not be their task to expand markets abroad and defend the property abroad of the exploiting classes. Soldiers will be allowed to organize and petition for the redress of grievances. Armed forces also include local police, under community control, as well as a greatly reduced prison system, based on the principle of restorative justice, and mainly for the protection of society from individuals inflicted with violent pathologies and criminal practices. Non-violent conflict resolution and community-based rehabilitation will be encouraged, but the need for some coercive means will remain for some time.

Carl Davidson is a national co-chair of the Committees of Correspondence for Democracy and Socialism, a national board member of the US Solidarity Economy Network, amd lead organizer of the Online University of the Left.

Getting Past Capitalism

By Cynthia Kaufman

In my book *Getting Past Capitalism*, I begin from the standpoint that capitalism is not a social totality that creates the mode of production that we inhabit. Rather it is a set of practices and processes that only partially define our reality. That is a crucial insight for imagining ways to challenge capitalism. Older anti-capitalist paradigms assumed a social totality, and they imagined an inevitable social rupture to lead us to the next phase of history. For the past 50 years many anti-capitalists have floundered when trying to figure out how to overthrow a totality without a belief in inevitability. What I argue is that if we stop looking at the problem as a totality to be done away with and focus rather on a set of problematic practices, we have a much clearer path forward. I also want to add that I think of alternatives as a multiplicity of possibilities, rather than as a totality called socialism.

Since capitalism is a set of practices promoted by people enjoying consumer pleasures; and a culture whose imagination has been colonized by consumerism; and a ruling class that can keep voting majorities dependent on pro-capitalist policies (as well as the power of violence) — how do we achieve a socially just and environmentally sustainable world?

There is no one core place to go to destroy capitalism. This is why it cannot be overthrown—why a coup against it won't work—and why even having a group of anti-capitalists take state power will not mean that it has been destroyed. Even countries like Bolivia, which have elected nominally anti-capitalist governments, have to deal with local wealthy landowners, pro-capitalist media, the transnational capitalist ruling class, transnational corporations, and a population dependent upon money to survive, all working to undermine their progress to a new economy.

Capitalist logics have woven themselves deeply into the social fabric. Much like the work done by public health officials in virus eradication, anti-capitalists must use a multiplicity of means and they must be ever vigilant against the continual reemergence of new ways that capitalist forms of destruction emerge.

Traditionally, anti-capitalists have focused on the state as the central locus of anti-capitalist activity, usually attempting to overthrow governments that support capitalism. But while states are an important locus of struggle, our analysis of how and when to fight states needs to be more nuanced than the idea of simply overthrowing the current group of people holding state power. When given a choice, people often vote for capitalism because they know that when capitalists suffer so do their employees. Going along with capitalism is in many people's short-term self-interest. States are often places where pro- and anti-capitalist interests vie for influence. Crucial to anti-capitalist struggle is challenging the conditions that make peoples' short-term self-interest dependent on capitalism, and that make them feel compelled to act according to short-term material interest rather than emotional, spiritual, environmental, or social interest.

In fighting against capitalism, decolonizing consciousness needs to be a huge part of our struggle. We need to, as individuals, reorient how we think of success and happiness in our lives, and we need to build cultural forms that spread this alternative way of experiencing the world.

Build Alternatives in the Present

It is important that we build alternative economic systems from right where we are, so that people can see that another world is possible and also so that we can build the new world. We make the road by walking and it takes actual power from the pro-capitalist forces.

Equally important, we need to actually work to challenge pro-capitalist forces. In order to protect their privilege, pro-capitalist forces will do everything they can to push for capitalism's extension and for more resources for the ruling class. They will do everything they can to destroy alternative models that might give people the impression that another world is possible. Pro-capitalist forces will also do everything they can to re-legitimize capitalism and to destroy or co-opt capitalism's opponents. They will use the media, economic sanctions, schools, propagandizing think tanks, cooptation of forms of funding, and a variety of forms of violence.

In addition to those active tools there is one tool in the pro-capitalist toolbox that works passively in capitalism's favor as a core structural component of a society dominated by capitalist processes: the economic dependency trap of capitalism. Working class people in a capitalist society need a wage to get the money they need to survive. In many places in the world, capitalism operates according to a basic compromise: workers will fight with capitalists over how much of the surplus will go to the workers and how much will go to the owners. They will fight for improved working conditions. People as a whole may fight through the state to constrain somewhat the operations of businesses. But everyone challenging capitalism in this way knows that their demands are limited by what a company can afford and still remain profitable, and by what a national economy can "afford" before policies that are good for the population begin to be "bad for the economy," that is, counterproductive to attracting capital for investment in the economy.

There are many ways that the economic dependency trap of capitalism functions without any pro-capitalist forces taking concerted action to impose it on working class people. It is simply true that a business pushed beyond profitability will cease to exist to employ people. And on a macro-scale, any policies that make investing undesirable for business will lead to unemployment. Once a society comes to have a large enough capitalist sector, the economic dependency trap thus functions passively as one of the most powerful tools favoring the interests of capitalism.

In addition to passively benefiting from this reality of capitalism, pro-capitalist forces will also make active use of the vulnerabilities created by the economic dependency trap through strategies such as the capital strike. This means that part of fighting capitalism is to minimize the economic dependency trap of capitalism.

I want to conclude with the 10 practical imperatives: To get past capitalism we need to:

1. Delegitimize capitalism. For many years those opposed to capitalism have been afraid to even name it.

2. We need to challenge pro capitalist cultural ideas with anti-capitalist art and media.

3. Live in ways that help you not to be a capitalist desiring subject. Find ways of generating pleasure and meaning in your life that do not rely on consumerism. Downshift your own expectations to the extent that pleasure comes from making and doing rather than buying. Attend to the quality of your relations with others and with the natural world.

4. Propagate anti-capitalist ways of understanding and measuring the economy. We need to develop ways to measure what is good for the economy that center on what is good for human and environmental development and creates a powerful opening for a radical transformation in values.

5. Challenge the major processes of capitalist reproduction in respectful coalition with others. Elaborate systems of social power, including mass media, the electoral and justice systems, state-sanctioned violence, and systemic discrimination, all reinforce capitalism in different ways. The biggest one of these right now is the fight against the Transpacific Partnership.

6. Develop larger strategies that will build synergy between small-scale and dispersed activities. As we engage in our dispersed tactics to push back capitalism, we need constantly to consider which of these strategies build most effectively toward a non-capitalist future. Work time reduction is an example of a specific goal that opens up all sorts of possibilities for a less capitalist world.

7. Make visible all of the ways that non-capitalism works well in our lives. We can foster the courage to criticize capitalism by promoting an understanding of all of the non-capitalist economic forms that are functioning well in our lives. We can draw attention to the systems of sharing and mutual support we all rely on, to the ways that state-run economic activity often works well, and to the ways that cooperatives function well.

8. Support the development of community controlled forms of capital. We can lessen our dependence upon the economic dependency trap of capitalism by supporting the efforts of non-capitalist entities such as local governments, community development projects, and cooperative businesses.

9. Build movements in ways that develop people's capacities. We need to develop organizational forms that will build in people a sense of commitment to a world without capitalism. We need what Gramsci called "pessimism of the intellect and optimism of the will," that is, we need to understand the seriousness of what we are up against while holding in our hearts and our intellects the belief that a world without capitalism is possible. Work with others, and attend to the ways that people are fed by those organizations. Make sure they feed people's sense of possibility.

10. Think strategically. We need to give up on the binary of reform versus revolution and look to build revolutionary reforms: actions that step-by-step begin to liberate us from capitalism. We need to avoid oversimplifying and looking for simple solutions, fulcrum points, or a black-and-white understanding of what we are doing. In all of your work, think about what you are doing and how it will add up to meaningful change. If we want to get past capitalism we need to be clever, flexible, perceptive, and brave.

Cynthia Kaufman is the Director of the Institute of Community and Civic Engagement, De Anza College, and author of "Getting Past Capitalism: History, Vision, Hope," 2012.

Book Review: 'A World To Build: New Paths Towards 21st Century Socialism.' By Marta Harnecker, Monthly Review Press, 2015

By Duncan McFarland

Marta Harnecker's new book is dedicated to the memory of Hugo Chavez and is rooted in Latin America's left turn politically and experiments in building socialism. One purpose of the author is to provide an inspiring vision, restoring the hope and promise of building socialism looking to the future. She succeeds by describing a socialism based on participatory democracy and workers' initiative and management, with an emphasis on decentralized decision making. It is a socialism that develops the rich, creative potentials of the whole person, uniting mental and physical labor, in harmony with nature. She describes a goal to "light the path" to win the hearts and minds of the great majority, an answer to the increasing failures of capitalism.

Harnecker accentuates the positive experiences in Latin America of global import. She also derives her vision from the works of Marx and Engels and their democratic and humanistic values. Her socialist vision, recognition of the importance of people's struggles in Latin America and promotion of Marxism, are all a great service in renewing a socialist movement and providing new inspiration to younger generations.

Harnecker identifies 20th century socialism with the Soviet Union, and she is relentless in her criticism of the centralized, top-down bureaucratic organization which excluded grassroots people from democratic participation, as they were relegated to cogs in the machine. So strong is her advocacy of decentralized decision-making and individual initiative in response to Soviet bureaucratization that she eventually clarifies that her call is for "non-anarchic decentralization impregnated with a spirit

Marta Harnecker

of solidarity." She then discusses the critical need for a new type of political instrument, rooted in the social movements to serve them.

Rooted in Latin America

There are also limits to Harnecker's analysis. Her book is based on the experiences of Latin America, the Soviet Union, Eastern Europe and the works of Marx. Harnecker is clearly writing to contribute to forward progress in Latin America. And, she clearly states that different countries have different paths to socialism. Yet her conclusions are not always qualified by her research. Recommendations for twenty-first century socialism sometimes have apparent relevance outside the region in the form of theoretical statements derived from numerous references to the work of Michael Lebowitz, a Canadian.

It is important for us to consider that her work is not based on an analysis of the US situation. For example, racism is barely touched on, yet is a critical component of the US struggle. Many would agree with the harsh critique of centralized power, but we also must understand that in the US, coordination and higher level organization of the super-fragmented left/socialist movement is a desperate need. Likewise, Harnecker calls for a broad progressive movement, including small businesses, essentially the progressive majority advocated by CCDS - but the working class role in providing left leadership for the broad coalition is not clarified or spelled out.

The assessment of Soviet history should carefully consider both positive and negative aspects, its contradictions and dilemmas. Could maximum decentralization have defeated the 17-country imperialist invasion during the Russian civil war, or the colossal attack of the Nazi war machine? There were Soviet accomplishments in promoting women's equality and providing basic services to the working class - should these policies be decided at a local level? Harnecker is ambiguous on Cuba and lacking in detail. She clearly admires and supports Cuba's defiance of US imperialism yet seems reluctant to acknowledge the role of the centralized party and state apparatus in maintaining Cuba's independence.

Centralization and decentralization are both necessary, a unity of opposites. The challenge is getting the right balance in the particular historical situation, which also changes. In citing Soviet failures, we do not want to disregard its successes or that it often served as a powerful force for the Left. The Soviet Union did establish an early model of socialism that sustained power for a protracted period, providing important lessons for present-day socialism to build upon. Ignoring this could lead to missing the positive contributions of other countries learning from the Russian revolution, and Lenin's leadership - or to disregarding the considerable historic accomplishments of the communist movement of the USA, lessons which can contribute to building 21st century socialism in this country .

The Ethics of Solidarity

Towards the end of the book Harnecker calls for "solidarity infused ethics" and highlights the "struggle to transform the people's consciousness by fighting against the cultural heritage of the past." She discusses the need for the political instrument to practice criticism and self-criticism. She emphasizes that individualism and backward ideas are deeply rooted in the inherited culture, an important educational challenge for 21st century socialism. In my view, these are important suggestions to counter fragmentation and build coordination in the US movement. The US dominant culture is largely derived from West European expansion in the 17th century, with its individualistic, Protestant character.

Harnecker's work will strengthen the new socialist movement in this country. She stresses the importance of an inspiring, democratic vision; the recent socialist developments in Latin America; the roots of Marxism; the need for a political instrument to build socialism; and the importance of political education and cultural change. Her assessment of the Soviet Union provides important conclusions but is also one-sided. We must preserve the positive accomplishments of the communist movement of the 20th century as well as discard its failures. These ideas must be applied creatively to help advance socialism in the US, a task now primarily for the younger generations with the assistance of the older comrades.

Duncan McFarland is a member of the CCDS national coordinating committee and chair of the Peace and Solidarity Committee CCDS.

Draft of an 8-Point Platform for Making a Major Breakthrough on 'Left Unity'

By Carl Davidson, Bill Fletcher, Jr. and Pat Fry

Introduction: The following eight-point proposal is designed to initiate both a discussion and a process. The points can be further refined, and subtracted from or added to. Given the scope of the challenges ahead of us, there is a certain degree of urgency, but it is also wise to take time to start off on a sound footing, uniting all who can be united. The main things it wants to bring into being at all levels—local, regional, national or in sectors—are common projects. Some of these already exist, such as the Left Labor Project in New York City, a good example of what we are advocating here. It brought together organizers from CCDS, CPUSA, DSA, Freedom Road Socialist Organization, and other independent left trade unionists and activists. Over a few years work, it was able to build a far wider alliance bringing together the city's labor organizations and allied social movements to bring out tens of thousands on May Day.

We know that many of us are already involved in a wide variety of projects. But is there any compelling reason we have to do this separately, behaving like a wheelbarrow full of frogs trying to win a common goal? A good case in point is Chuy Garcia's mayoral campaign in Chicago. Wouldn't this campaign be better served if we worked together in a planned way to draw in and skillfully deploy even more forces? Or take the labor-community alliance projects building solidarity for labor strikes or the campaign for an increase in the minimum wage? We can all make a long list here, but the core idea should be apparent, at least for starters, and we invite your responses and queries.

1. We need something new. The left is not likely to find critical mass through mergers of existing groups, although any such events would be positive. But a new formation to which all would be equally cooperative in a larger project—call it a Left Front or Left Alliance—would have a greater impact. Groups participating in it could retain whatever degree of autonomy they desire, such as keeping their own newspapers, national committees, local clubs meeting separately, and so on. Every group involved can exercise its own independence and initiative, to the degree it finds necessary. But all would be striving in common to help the overall project succeed. While the US situation is not strictly comparable, the Front de Gauche in France, Die Linke in Germany, PODEMOS in Spain and Syriza in Greece serve as examples.

2. We need a 'project based' common front. At the grassroots level, it would be comprised of joint projects—electoral, union organizing, campaigns against the far right, against climate change, for a living wage or reducing student debt, for opposing war, racism, sexism and police violence, and many others. The existing left groups in a factory, a neighborhood, a city or a campus, would be encouraged to advance the joint projects.

3. We need a 'critical mass' at the core that is both young, working class and diverse. While people from all demographics are welcome, the initial core has to be largely drawn from the Millennials, those born after 1980 or so. And the core also has to be a rainbow of nationalities with gender equity, and well-connected to union and working class insurgencies. If the initial core at the beginning is too 'white' or too '1968ers', it will not be a pole with the best attractive power for a growing new generation of socialist and radical minded activists.

4. We need a common aspiration for socialism. That's what makes us a 'Left Front or Left Alliance' rather than a broader popular front or people's coalition. We are strongly supportive of these wider coalitions and building the left is not done in isolation from them. But we also see the wisdom in the concept: the stronger the core, the broader the front. Moreover we do not require a unified definition on what socialism is; only that a larger socialist pole makes for an even wider, deeper and more sustainable common front of struggle.

5. We do not need full agreement on strategy. A few key concepts—the centrality of fighting white supremacy, the intersection of race, class and gender, the alliance and merger of the overall workers movement and the movements of the communities of the oppressed—will do. We can also agree on cross-class alliances focused on critical targets: new wars, climate disaster, the far right and the austerity schemes imposed by finance capital. Additional elements, perspectives, nuances and 'shades of difference' can be debated, discussed and adjusted in the context of ongoing struggle

6. We need a flexible but limited approach to elections. We can affirm that supporting our own or other candidates is a matter of tactics to be debated case-by-case, and not a matter of 'principle' that would exclude ever voting for any particular Democrat, Green or Socialist. We see the importance for social movements to have an electoral arm that presses and fights for their agenda within government bodies.

7. We need to be well embedded in grassroots organizations. Especially important are the organizations of the working class and in the communities of the oppressed—unions and worker centers, civil rights and women's rights, youth and students, peace and justice, churches and communities of faith, cooperatives and other groups tied to the solidarity economy, environmental justice, and other community-based NGOs and nonprofits.

8. We need to be internationalists. But we do not have to require support for any particular countries or bloc of countries and national liberation movements, past or present. But we do oppose the wars of aggression, occupations and other illicit interventions of 'our own' ruling class, along with the hegemonism, 'superpower mentality' and Great Power chauvinism it promotes. That is the best way we can promote world peace and practice solidarity and assistance to forces beyond our borders.

Carl Davidson and Pat Fry are national co-chairs of Committees of Correspondence for Democracy and Socialism. Bill Fletcher Jr. is a member of several socialist organizations and author of 'They're Bankrupting Us! And 20 Other Myths about Unions.' Comments can be sent to carld717@gmail.com

Bus/Taxi Coop in Cuba. Cuba is poised to be the first country in the world to have cooperatives make up a major portion of its economy. It is a laboratory for a new society.

Cooperative Cuba

By Cliff DuRand

Cuba is engaged in a fundamental reshaping of its society. Calling it a renovation of socialism or a renewal of socialism, the country is reforming the economic system away from the state socialist model adopted in the 1970s toward something quite new. This is not the first time Cuba has undertaken significant changes, but this promises to be deeper than previous efforts, moving away from that statist model. Fidel confessed in 2005 that "among the many errors that we committed, the most serious error was believing that someone knew how to build socialism." That someone, of course, was the Soviet Union. So, Cuba is still trying to figure out for itself how to build socialism.

To understand the current renovation it is important to distinguish between ownership and possession of property. The productive resources of society are to remain under state ownership in the name of all the people. Reforms do not change the ownership system. Reforms are changing the management system, bringing managerial control closer to those who actually possess property. So while the state will continue to own, greater autonomy will be given to those who possess that property. In effect, Cuba is embracing the principle of subsidiarity, which holds that decisions should be made at the lowest level feasible and higher levels should give support to the local. This means more enterprise autonomy in state enterprises and it means cooperatives outside of the state.

It is expected that in the next couple years the non-state sector is expected to provide 35% of the employment. Along with foreign and joint ventures, the non-state sector as a whole will contribute an estimated 45% of the gross domestic product (PIB). Hopefully, coops will become a dominant part of that non-state sector.

Cooperatives

Already 83% of agricultural land is in coops. Much of that has been in the UBPCs (Basic Units of Cooperative Production) formed in the 1990s out of the former state farms. But these were not true cooperatives since they still came under the control of state entities. Now they are being given the autonomy to become true coops.

Even more significantly, new urban coops are being established in services and industry. Two hundred and twenty-two experimental urban coops are to be opened in 2013; as of July 1, 124 have been formed in agricultural markets, construction, and transportation. A big expansion in this number is expected in 2014.

In December 2012 the National Assembly passed an urban coop law that establishes the legal basis for these new coops. Here are some of its main provisions:

- A coop must have at least 3 members, but can have as many as 60 or more. One vote per socio. As self-governing enterprises, coops are to set up their own internal democratic decision making structures.
- Coops are independent of the state. They are to respond to the market. This is to overcome the limits that hampered some agricultural coops in the past.
- Coops can do business with state and private enterprises. They will set their own prices in most cases, except where there are prices established by the state.
- Some coops will be conversions of state enterprises, e.g. restaurants. They can have 10-year renewable leases for use of the premises, paying no rent in the first year if improvements are made. Others will be start-up coops.

- There will be second degree coops which are associations of other coops.
- Capitalization will come from bank loans, a new Finance Ministry fund for coops and member contributions. Member contributions are treated as loans (not equity) and do not give additional votes. Loans are to be repaid from profits.
- Coops are to pay taxes on profits and social security for socios.
- Distribution of profits is to be decided by socios after setting aside a reserve fund.
- Coops may hire wage labor on a temporary basis (up to 90 days). After 90 days a temporary worker must be offered membership or let go. Total temporary worker time cannot exceed 10% of the total work days for the year. This gives coops flexibility to hire extra workers seasonally or in response to increased market demands, but prevents significant collective exploitation of wage labor.

This is a big step forward for Cuba. Since 1968 the state has sought to run everything from restaurants to barber shops and taxis. Some were done well, many were not. One problem was worker motivation. Decisions were made higher up and as state employees, workers enjoyed job security even with poor performance. However, their pay was low. Now as socios in cooperatives they will have incentives to make the business a success. The coop is on its own to either prosper or go under. Each member's income and security depends on the collective. And each has the same voting right in the General Assembly where coop policy is to be made. Coops combine material and moral incentives, linking individual interest with a collective interest. Each socio prospers only if all prosper.

Remittances: Much of the start-up capital from members is likely to come from remittances sent by relatives living abroad. This is a good way to harness for the social good some of the $2.455 billion of remittance money (2012 figures) that comes into Cuba. Although 62.4% of the population receive remittances, the bulk of this money is likely to come to whiter Cubans. As a result Black Cubans will end up being underrepresented in this sector of the economy. In the long run, this presents social dangers.

Recommendation: Preferential bank lending policies can avoid this problem. Cuba does not need to adopt race based affirmative action policies to correct this imbalance. Banks can give preference in their lending policies to those coops that lack funding from remittances. To each according to his need.

State plan: If coops are truly autonomous, how can this sector of the economy be articulated with planning? Guideline #1 says the socialist planning system is to remain "the principle means to direct the national economy."

How can market and plan work together? In addition to responding to the market, coops are also charged (by charter?) with a "social object." In addition, local entities can also request that they assist in specific social projects. Their participation is voluntary. This applies to individual coops.
But beyond this, the investment function can be used to direct the development of this sector. Bank lending priorities can be based on state development plans.

The model for economic democracy developed by US philosopher David Schweickart shows how this can operate. In *After Capitalism,* [1] Schweickart envisions a society made up of democratically managed cooperatives exchanging goods and services in a free market. But the allocation of investment capital is made by government bodies at national, regional and local levels based on social criteria democratically decided upon. Something like this would seem to fit well the new economy developing in Cuba today.

Coops are recognized as a socialist form of organization in the Guidelines or *lineamientos*. In part, this is because they foster a social consciousness. By bringing people together in their daily worklife in democratically self-managed organizations, coops nurture the democratic personality and the human being is more fully developed. This point has been strongly advocated by Cuban economist Camila Piñeiro Harnecker. She argues that coops "promote the advancement of democratic values, attitudes and habits (equality, responsibility, solidarity, tolerance for different opinions, communication, consensus building)." [2] Coops are little schools of democracy in which the new socialist person can thrive, more so than was possible under state socialism. [3] Thus coops spontaneously generate at the base of society momentum toward that society of associated producers that is the aim of socialism. Coops are the kind of institution that can make socialism irreversible by embedding its practices in daily life.

Private Businesses

The other component of the non-state sector is made up of private businesses. These small and medium sized private businesses are called self-employment or *cuentapropistas*. While limited areas of self employment were opened up in the 1990s (e.g. *paladares*), this was expanded to 178 occupations in 2011. In part, this was designed to quickly absorb the large number of redundant state employees that were to be dismissed. It also allowed underground activities that had flourished since the Special Period to come out into the open and operate legally where they could be licensed, regulated and taxed.

The acceptance of small private businesses signifies that the leadership recognizes that a petty bourgeoisie is compatible with socialism. As it is often said, the state cannot do everything. Contrary to a common claim in the US media, this is not the beginning of capitalism. The Guidelines say that accumulation of wealth is to be avoided. This means the petty bourgeoisie will not be allowed to grow into a big bourgeoisie, a capitalist class.

Unlike coops which nurture a social consciousness, private businesses foster individualism. Self-interest becomes the primary concern of private businesses. For that reason the petty bourgeoisie is a decidedly non-socialist class. While its existence is allowed, its growth should not be encouraged where coops can do the job instead.

Unlike the *paladares* which could employ only family members, these private businesses can hire others as well. While this is also called self-employment, in reality it is wage labor. While the private exploitation of wage labor is widely understood to be incompatible with socialism (as well as in violation of the Cuban constitution), it is accepted as necessary to quickly absorb surplus workers.

In recent years, small private businesses have been the fastest growing element in the Cuban economy. If they were to come to make up a sizable portion of the non-state sector, they could easily acquire significant political influence, moving Cuba away from socialism. This is because class power is fundamentally rooted in the significance a class has in the economy as a whole and thus the dependence other classes and groups have on its success.

For that reason, the continued development of socialism requires that coops rather than private businesses come to make up the bulk of the non-state sector. That is likely to be the case for several reasons.

- Coops are favored by the state in terms of tax policy and loan policies.
- In direct competition between coops and private businesses, coops often are in more advantageous positions, e.g. state restaurants that convert to coop restaurants generally have better locations than private restaurants.
- Labor efficiency and productivity is high in coops due to the greater incentives for socios.

Recommendation: In the long run it would be desirable to convert many private businesses into coops so all who are employed there can enjoy the benefits equally (no exploitation) and participate in decision making (democracy). This could be done by restrictions on the size of private businesses, tax incentives for conversion, and political organizing of their wage labor force.

Role of CTC (Central de Trabajadores de Cuba)

In view of the new and growing diversity among Cuba's workers, the role of its labor movement needs to be rethought. Under state socialism the CTC represented the interest of the working class as a whole in the councils of government. Unlike unions in a capitalist society which represent workers in an industry or particular workplaces in an adversarial relationship with capital, in state socialism the state and the working class are considered to be united in their interests. It is for this reason that the CTC has been given a central position in the political structure. Its role is not to represent workers in negotiations with their employers, but to be their voice in making public policy in a socialist society.

Previously only 9% of employment was in the non-state sector. Now it is 22% and is expected to grow to 35%. This raises new questions for the labor movement. Reportedly, 80% of cuentapropistas have joined unions. How can the CTC represent the interests of those cuentapropistas who are private business owners? The petty bourgeoisie has interests different from the working class (even though they do work in their businesses). How can CTC at the same time represent the interests of the cuentapropistas who are in fact the wage laborers they employ (and exploit)?

And how can the CTC represent the interests of cooperative socios given the fact that they are at once both owners and workers? While the CTC could advance socialism by advocating for the cooperative sector as a whole over against the private business sector it might be more suitable to have a separate federation of cooperatives to carry out this role. It might also take on an entrepreneurial role for cooperatives, doing market research, organizing workers for new start-up coops, providing training in self-management, and even monitoring coops to ensure compliance with their own self-governance processes.

21st Century Socialism

The project called 21st Century Socialism has been associated primarily with the Bolivarian Revolution in Venezuela. It is an attempt to reinvent socialism after the collapse of the state socialism that characterized the 20th century. In Venezuela this has involved using state power to promote cooperatives and communal councils at the base of society as seeds of a future socialism. Social transformation is constructed both from above and from below. [4] In Venezuela this is taking place in what is still overwhelmingly a capitalist society. In Cuba we see a very similar process in the context of a state socialist society. Here the state is also promoting cooperatives, relaxing administrative control over enterprises and decentralizing governmental power to the local level. Both see the empowerment of associations at the base of society and the active participation of working people in directing their affairs as key to building the new socialism. In the Venezuelan case this is seen as eventually replacing the existing bourgeois state with a new communal state, the beginnings of which are being constructed by associations of communal councils.

In the case of Cuba, resistance to this dispersal of power away from the state is reportedly coming from the state bureaucracy itself. Some see this as motivated by the self interest of an entrenched bureaucratic class that will block Cuba's reforms. Others see the resistance as due to bureaucratic habits that are slow to change. In that case it can be overcome by a change of mentality.[5] There is also bureaucratic resistance in Venezuela. That is why power and resources are being sent directly to communal councils, effectively by-passing traditional channels. Something like that same strategy is being used in Cuba as some taxes are being collected at the local level rather than nationally to be distributed downward. This then shifts the capacity to initiate action to the local level, a far cry from the vertical structure of state socialism.

Democratically self-governing cooperatives are an essential feature of 21st century socialism. They empower the associated producers in their daily work, giving them some control over their lives. At the same time these little schools of democracy are the soil in which the new socialist person will thrive, more so than was possible under state socialism. And with that it becomes possible to envision the state eventually withering away as society comes more and more under the direction of a truly civil society, or what Marx called the associated producers.

Conclusion

Cuba is poised to be the first country in the world to have cooperatives make up a major portion of its economy. It is a laboratory for a new society. Those who are implementing the Guidelines are aware that they are redesigning society and approach the challenge in an experimental way. The new urban coops are being set up as experiments. As difficulties emerge lessons are to be learned so as to improve the process as it goes along.

One difficulty is already evident: the need for education in cooperativism.[6]. Previous experience in the UBPC agricultural coops showed that workers were not practiced in democratic decision making. Nor did the coops have the autonomy necessary for them to feel they were really in control. The UBPCs were actually under the control of state enterprises, such as the sugar centrals. Now for the first time they are being given real autonomy.

Likewise, the workers in urban state enterprises now being cooperativized have deeply established habits of compliance with higher authority. Under state socialism decisions came from higher up. It was a structure that bred passivity. That is part of the "change in mentality" so often talked about these days that needs to take place.

Many years ago Cuban philosopher Olga Fernandez pointed out to me that under the model of socialism Cuba had adopted, rather than the state withering away, it was civil society that was withering away. Today's renovation of socialism is an effort to rejuvenate civil society, to construct a socialist civil society. Cooperatives may be a key link in that rejuvenation that can sustain Cuba on its way to a society run by the associated producers. If it can succeed, it will be of world historical importance.

Notes

[1] David Schweickart, *After Capitalism* (Rowman and Littlefield, 2nd edition 2011), pp. 47-58.
[2] Camila Piñeiro Harnecker, "Las cooperatives en el Nuevo modelo economico cubano" http://rebelion.org/mostrar.php?tipo=5&id=Camila%20Pi%F1eiro%20Harnecker&inicio=0, also Cooperativas y socialismo: Una mirada desde Cuba (La Habana: *Editorial Caminos*, 2011).
[3] Michael A. Lebowitz, *The Contradictions of Real Socialism* (Monthly Review Press, 2012).
[4] Dario Azzellini, "The Communal State: Communal Councils, Communes, and Workplace Democracy" *NACLA Report on the Americas* (Summer 2013), pp. 25-30.
[5] Olga Fernandez "Socialist Transition in Cuba: Economic Adjustments and Socio-political Challenges" *Latin American Perspectives* (forthcoming).
[6] This has been emphasized by Beatriz Diaz of FLACSO in "Cooperatives in the Enhancement of the Cuban Economic Model: The Challenge of Cooperative Education" *Latin American Perspectives* (forthcoming). Camila Piñeiro Harnecker has proposed establishment of a special department to train coop members for their new role. Op. cit.

Cliff DuRand is affiliated with the Center for Global Justice, San Miguel de Allende, Mexico

LeftRoots: Towards A Transformational Strategy

By N'Tanya Lee, Cinthya Muñoz, Maria Poblet, Josh Warren-White and Steve Williams

We are living in times of great instability and crisis. Everywhere there are troubling signs of collapse: mass shootings; widespread unemployment; potentially irreversible ecological devastation; and the consolidation of wealth into fewer and fewer hands. The interpenetrating crises within the economic system, the ecological system, and the system of empire are pushing the 1% to implement massive austerity programs, militarization, and further disenfranchisement of oppressed communities. But not everything is gloom and doom. In the face of the ruling class' savage attacks, heroic struggles are breaking out around the world against the manifestations of imperialism, capitalism, white supremacy, and patriarchy.

While these crises have called the legitimacy of ruling class hegemony into question, it is by no means guaranteed that popular forces will succeed in rescuing the world from the tyranny of the 1%. We are living in a period in which, as Antonio Gramsci once observed, the old order is dying while the new phase is still struggling to be born.

Even though the ruling class faces instability and internal strife, they are armed to the teeth and are committed to holding onto power at any cost. What happens in the next period of history will determine the future of the planet and humankind.

From Resistance to Strategy Development

In response to the worsening conditions in our communities, and driven by a deep desire to change the systems that have made conditions so bad for our people, many social movement activists have taken up the work of organizing resistance. This work is critical. But it's not enough. We need our fights to add up to something beyond resistance.

So often activists in reform fights say, "I don't think that we'll ever achieve liberation, but I want to do what I can." The problem with this attitude is that it closes us off to seeing and seizing opportunities to take unimagined leaps forward. After all, who would have dreamed in the beginning of 2011 that by the end of the year people across the country would be occupying public spaces denouncing the tyranny of the 1%? Or, that fast food workers across the country would be walking off their jobs to demand a living wage? Or, that undocumented youth would be intentionally getting detained so they could organize resistance inside detention centers? Or that there would be a  well organized national mass movement against police violence growing out of another police murder of a Black youth?

Holding onto the hope that we could win, that we could radically transform society is difficult, but vital. That hope and audacity can change the way that we organize, fight, and build movements. The problem is that it is almost impossible to keep hope alive if we don't have a plan to win.

Strategy is one of the fundamental building blocks for all successful revolutionary movements. In revolutionary periods throughout history, well-developed strategy has enabled organizers to cohere different sectors of society into a unified movement of movements that was able to defy the odds and transform society. Each of these strategies were as unique as the conditions from which they emerged, and the most successful evolved over time as those conditions changed.

There are no successful cookie-cutter strategies. What worked in one place, at one time, will not necessarily work in another. That said, while every strategy must grow out of its own particular time, place, and conditions, there are some common features of successful revolutionary strategies. Broadly speaking, they are:

- Articulate a vision of a transformed society;
- Examine the characteristics and conditions of society's social and economic groupings;
- Project a revolutionary historic bloc by assessing which social sectors have the most vested interest in transforming society, which might support that vision, and which have the power to carry out that transformation;
- Evaluate the balance of power between organizations and the interests those organizations represent;

- Assess the cultural, social, economic, and political hegemony;
- Name collective goals to be achieved by advancing the larger strategy; and
- Identify key fights in which to concentrate forces.

The Need for the Left

Historically, it has been Leftists from different resistance struggles that have come together to forge a broader strategy for liberation. Although Left forces in many parts of the world are taking bold steps to navigate the twists and turns of the current period with effective strategy, such a Left does not exist in the United States today. There are important Left organizations and formations in this country, but a coherent and audacious Left in the United States will have to be re-constituted if this role is to be fulfilled.

The task of re-constituting a radical and relevant Left in the United States faces many serious challenges. Despite these challenges, there are reasons to be hopeful. Along with mass organizations rooted amongst exploited and oppressed sectors, a successful revolutionary movement today will require one or many Left formations which learn from the errors of 20th century Left organizations. In order to be successful this Next Left will need to be:

- Strongly rooted amongst key social sectors and geographical regions in order to accurately ground its analysis of the objective and subjective conditions;
- Capable of strengthening existing social movements. It will need to be respectful of popular organizations and movements, relating to them not merely as conveyor belts or competitors, but as partners which have unique and valuable contributions that are needed to advance the struggle and pave the way for the emergence of a free society;
- Able to bring the distinct demands of various social movements together into a single political project in ways that those movements see themselves authentically represented. This requires the ability and desire to listen to the wisdom that exists amongst comrades, other activists, and unorganized people;
- Capable of identifying key fronts of struggle where collective action can shift the balance of power and create new openings; and
- Constantly searching for opportunities to expand popular protagonism and democratic participation — both inside Left organizations and society in general.

This is a different kind of Left than the self-proclaimed vanguard model that was so prevalent in the 20th century. New types of Left formations are beginning to prosper in countries like Greece, South Africa, Venezuela, and Bolivia. These political instruments are helping to establish new models and new practices that we have a lot to learn from, despite our different context in the United States.

Developing grounded strategy for liberation and developing cadre capable of carrying out that strategy are two central tasks of building a liberatory movement of movements in the United States today.

Leaning Forward

History is not flat. It ebbs and flows like the tide. Recent events in Egypt are a prime example of this. After decades of isolated workers' strikes and anti-police brutality organizing, a movement that mobilized millions of people erupted. In a matter of weeks, the people of Egypt deposed a US-backed dictator who had been in power for decades. The tasks for revolutionaries change depending on the nature of the period in which they're working. During ebbs, we engage in fights, build our forces, and prepare to advance. Most struggles during these periods take place within a political context that is not to our advantage. During flows, we advance. We surge forward. These periods of flow often correspond to structural crises and offer revolutionaries opportunities to gain ground and shift the terrain for future struggle.

We believe we are in a period of flow in which crisis is likely to expand. Instability will become the norm. In response, the ruling class will likely exert their power through violence and intimidation more than through concessions and persuasion. This will lead to more action from both the Right wing as well as popular forces. Global instability will allow many nations outside of the First World to explore building alternatives outside of US imperialism. This will be especially true in the Global South.

These moments are when revolutionaries can begin to make possible what until recently seemed impossible. These moments hold untold challenges and opportunities. In order to advance, revolutionaries must be prepared. History suggests that progressive advance will require a strong and skilled Left. In order to help meet that need we have begun building LeftRoots, a national formation of Left social movement organizers and activists who want to connect grassroots struggles to a strategy to win liberation for all people and the planet.

We do not yet have a fully developed strategy, but based on a cursory assessment of the current conditions and the imbalance of political forces in the United States, LeftRoots has developed an outline of some of the tasks needed to strengthen the position of the Left, weaken the position of the Right, and win the trust and loyalty of important sectors of U.S. society:
- **Build popular organizations.** Mass organizations are the basic build-

ing block of all revolutionary movements. These organizational forms allow people to rebuild community; to make connections between their own struggles, the struggles of their neighbors, and their connections to the system; and they allow people to take collective action. Too often, these organizations have been seen as conveyor belts feeding information and resources to more strategic parts of the movement. We believe that these organizations must be vital participants in any liberation movement. Popular organizations generate energy, innovation, and wisdom that must be respected and supported.

- **Wage counter-hegemonic fights.** As the crisis continues to deepen, people will rise up and take action, calling for change. In different places these actions will have different demands. It is the responsibility of a renewed Left to support and strengthen those fights, but Leftists need to be mindful of not falling into the pitfalls of populism. The next Left must seek to make what seems impossible now possible in the future. This Left must offer analysis, suggestions, and material support with the aim of deepening those fights where possible to undermine ruling class hegemony and to nurture a liberatory hegemony.

- **Build alternatives.** In addition to participating in and supporting popular struggles, a renewed Left must engage in and support efforts to build alternative institutions and practices that could help serve as some of the building blocks of a post-capitalist society. In all of these activities we must work democratically, showing respect, accountability, tolerance, and love for the people and the planet.

- **Engage in the Battle of Ideas.** A renewed Left must ground itself in a vision of a free society. We call this vision 21st Century Socialism in an effort to signal the need to break from capitalism and to avoid repeating the errors of the 20th century socialist experiments. This vision will inform the development of a clear strategy of how to get there. The Left must also engage in the Battle of Ideas. We must present our vision of a free society in ways that connect with people's very real frustrations with capitalist society and their ambitions for a better future. Along with the frontline struggles and alternative institutions, this work will lay the basis for a new common sense.

- **Forge a revolutionary social bloc.** Any successful effort to challenge and build alternatives to the capitalist, racist, and sexist world order will involve millions of people around the world. The strategic alliance between the working class and communities of color form the two wings of the bloc that can lead a successful challenge to the ruling class in the United States. Building democratic organizations rooted in working class communities of color provides the greatest guarantee that the interests of these sectors is at the center of the perspectives, programs, and demands of the movement. Because their interests demand an end to the tyranny of patriarchy, white supremacy, capitalism, and imperialism, building organizations rooted in these sectors is of strategic importance. However, the Left's attention cannot focus on these sectors exclusively. The Left must cultivate a vision, organizational fronts, and demands that forge a new identity, a new social bloc that sees its interests as being served best by an alternative to the existing tyranny of the 1%. Winning over and engaging other sectors of society — without betraying the interests of the most exploited and oppressed sectors both here in the U.S. and around the world — is one of the central strategic tasks of a renewed Left.

• **Connect with struggles around the globe.** Any liberatory movement based in the United States must recognize the imperial privilege that this country has and continues to profit from. Justice and liberation cannot be achieved at the expense of the global community. International solidarity and global equity must be a driving principle of any liberation movement. The next Left will look to build connections to social movements around the world and to link our local struggles to the efforts of other activists struggling on different terrain towards our common objectives.

• **Renew our movement culture.** To make such a revolutionary project possible, we need a renewed Left culture based on respect for political and ideological pluralism. This is deeply connected to the dialectical process of breaking from the alienation so pervasive in the capitalist system. As we struggle to transform society, we must also struggle to transform ourselves. This will happen through conscious work at individual and collective levels, just as it will happen through collective struggles for human solidarity as we recover parts of ourselves that have been long atrophied in an environment of consumerism and individualism.

• **Build democratic participation and revolutionary protagonism.** The capitalist democracy promoted by the U.S. empire is a hallow perversion. Democratic protagonism rejects the idea that democracy is simply about one magical moment of decision-making. Through our exposure to systems, we all learn and develop particular skills and attitudes. Social relations under capitalism undermine and diminish our capacities. On the other hand, participatory democracy takes into account all of the steps leading up to the making of the decision, thereby promoting people to be protagonists, the makers of history. As Karl Marx noted, the key to revolutionary practice is not simply being in a different circumstance, but also in helping to make that changed situation. The Next Left must take up different practices and procedures to develop everyone's capacities so that we can all play leading roles in shaping the decisions, workplaces, communities, and world in which we live.

- **Deepen our capacity to respond to ruptures.** The first years of this decade have witnessed an unprecedented level of ecological catastrophe, social upheaval and popular mobilization. Much of this action is a direct response to social, economic, and political contradictions and the ruling class' self-serving attempts to manage those contradictions — since it is not in their interests to fully resolve the contradictions. As long as these social, economic, and ecological contradictions continue to grow, more upsurges and mobilizations are likely to occur. The task for a renewed and reinvigorated Left will be to support and offer facilitative leadership in the midst of those reactions. Individual Leftists acting independently cannot accomplish this task. Nimble and coherent, collective action of Leftists multiplies and amplifies the impact of social movements and of the Left so that crisis can be transformed into opportunity; the opportunity to begin making real our vision of a more just, equal, sustainable, and protagonistic world.

While this outline marks a particular approach to building a liberatory movement, we recognize that it is just an outline. It is not a strategy. Within this outline, there are a lot of unanswered questions: what is the class structure of US society? Which classes and social groups have the power and potential to lead and participate in a historic bloc for liberatory transformation? What regions have the most potential to advance the struggle? What might be the role of rural-urban alliances in a liberation movement? How does the re-emergence of the racist right, the expanding role of state-sponsored infiltration and criminalization impact movement building efforts? Given the financial crises impacting state and local governments, what campaigns and targets give us the best possibility to advance? The list goes on.

Ultimately, more research and analysis will be necessary in order to ground our analysis in the real conditions and class structure of the US empire, and we believe that by doing this work, we will be able to make this outline a strategic tool with goals, objectives, and criteria that can help strengthen the struggle for a free society.

LeftRoots is not acting alone to achieve these objectives. We are both a project and an organization. As a project, LeftRoots aims to work with others to help nurture the re-emergence of an ideologically sharp, tactically adept, and strategically clear Left that can help spark and be of service to massive social movements confronting and building alternatives to imperialism, capitalism, white supremacy and patriarchy.

As an organization, LeftRoots is a political home for a grouping of social movement Leftists that we consider to be key to the re-emergence of the Next left in the United States.

Building Beyond the Social Movement Left

As we've discussed, any successful revolutionary movement will involve conscious and organized Left forces. It is equally important that the Left include the participation and leadership of those from the very social sectors that make up the leading forces in the liberation struggle: working class people, people of color, women, queer, gender queer, and young people.

Clearly, this is not what the self-identified Left looks like right now. For the Left to be successful will require a radical shift in who sees themselves as a part of it. Though we are far from this reimagined Left, there are hundreds of Leftists out there, many of us playing key roles in social movements rooted in the popular sectors that will play a central role if the US Left is to expand its power and influence.

These Leftists who are deeply engaged in social movements must play a leading role in renewing and reshaping the Left in the United States. This will not be easy since social movement and base organizing work are relentless and can be all-consuming, but it's necessary. Leftists in social movements are uniquely positioned to bring together the lessons and experiences from various frontline struggles to expand on old ideas and practices and develop innovative new ones.

Many do not see the revolutionary potential of the social movement Left. We are like bees of the movement world. Many flight experts don't understand how bees actually fly. According to their calculations, their wings are too small to be able to carry their relatively large bodies. Undeterred by the naysayers, bees fly around and play a critical role in supporting the ecosystem. Bees cross-pollinate. They carry pollen in the same way that social movement Leftists so often cross over the silos that constrain our movement work, bringing information and lessons from one movement to another.

Bees are social creatures. They draw their strength from acting in cooperation with the other bees in their colony. One of the most dangerous impacts of the increased use of pesticides is that many of those chemicals are drugging bees to such an extent that they are not able to find their way back to their hives. Isolated and separated from their homes, bees are dying off in alarming numbers.

Due to many different reasons including the impacts of COINTELPRO, the neoliberal assault and the weakening of the global left, social movement Leftists in the United States have been trying to figure out answers on our own, hoping our efforts would add up to something more. But isolated and unable to collectivize our power and impact, we have come up against the limitations of nonprofits and the trade union movement.

LeftRoots is building a political home for social movement Leftists in the United States to come together to build a collective identity and to develop transformational strategy that can help unleash the power of the people. This, we hope will contribute to sharpening the Left edge of social movements and reinvigorating the Left in general.

Footnote:

'Protagonism' is a term that we first came across in the work of Marta Harnecker who noted its usage amongst social movement activists throughout Latin America. We have adopted the use of the term within LeftRoots even though there is no direct translation in English because, like no other term we've come across, 'protagonism' names an approach that has the potential to strengthen social movements inside the United States. The concept builds from the literary term 'protagonist' which refers to a character who takes ownership over her destiny and drives the narrative forward by taking action. In a similar vein, we understand protagonism to be the democratic engagement which builds our individual and collective capacities for transformative change and, in doing so, combats our fundamental alienation from the means of production, from the products of our labor, from each other, and from ourselves.

N'Tanya Lee, Cinthya Muñoz, Maria Poblet, Josh Warren-White and Steve Williams are affiliated with the LeftRoots Coordinating Committee

CCDS Statement on Solidarity with Vietnam

April 30, 2015 marked the 40th Anniversary of the end of the war in Vietnam and its total liberation from US imperialism and foreign occupation. For ten years, from 1965-1975, Vietnam was at the center of world attention as a small but proud country that fought the most powerful imperialist military power in history and won.

The price was very high. Three million to four million Vietnamese were killed, millions more maimed, and another 5 million people poisoned with Agent Orange. A massive anti-war movement, in the US and world-wide, grew during the war years to support the Vietnamese people, to put social, economic and political pressure on the US war makers to withdraw funds and troops from the war.

Since the war's end, Vietnam has overcome tremendous obstacles to become one of the fastest growing economies in the world. With nearly full employment, Vietnam has made among the greatest improvements in raising living standards and eradicating poverty of any country in the world.

Vietnam is also a leader in increasing life expectancy, advancing education, electing women and minorities to government at all levels, and developing a rich humanistic culture, all components in building a vibrant socialist society.

The Committees of Correspondence for Democracy and Socialism sends warm fraternal greetings to the people of Vietnam, its government, the Communist Party of Vietnam, the Vietnam Women's Union, the Vietnam-USA Society, the Vietnam Association for Victims of Agent Orange, and the many mass people's organizations on the 40th Anniversary of its total liberation, and wishes Vietnam and its people many future successes. Many of the leaders and members of CCDS were leaders and activists in the US anti-war movement over 40 years ago. We continue to express our solidarity with Vietnam and pledge to continue our work for the victims of Agent Orange, and to advance the friendship between our two peoples.

40th Anniversary of End of the War in Vietnam: A Photo Essay

April 30, 2015 marked the 40th anniversary of the total liberation of Vietnam from US war, occupation, and imperialist rule. The victors were the Vietnamese people, who played the leading role in this heroic decades-long struggle that was filled with immeasurable sacrifices. From the early 1960s, the Vietnamese liberation movement won the hearts and minds of peace and justice loving people in the United States and around the world. Millions of people here and abroad joined the world-wide anti-war movement in support of the Vietnamese and to work to end the war.

This year, 2015, the US government has embarked on a national program, not to commemorate Vietnam on its 40 years of independence, but instead to commemorate the war years by re-writing history. The US government's focus is to honor Vietnam veterans and their families, and all organizations that supported the war effort, implying that their sacrifices were for an honorable cause. The cause was not honorable.

Absent is the real history of the war, the reasons for US involvement, the terrible killing of 3 million Vietnamese and the destruction of much of their country. We will not hear about the US corporate drive to get cheap raw materials, cheap labor, new markets, and total political control of South East Asia at the point of a gun. We will not hear about the carpet bombings that killed Vietnamese men, women and children indiscriminately and destroyed villages and towns, laid waste to rice paddies and other agricultural lands, and poisoned the water, food, land and people of Vietnam with Agent Orange. We will not hear about the US government's successful effort to sabotage the 1954 Geneva Accord-mandated elections to re-unite Vietnam in 1956, after the defeat of French colonialism in Vietnam, because as president Eisenhower admitted later, "possibly 80% of the population would have voted for the Communist Ho Chi Minh," and not the US government hand-picked man it had installed in power in southern Vietnam.

Nor will we hear about the massive anti-war movement in the US, the millions of Americans who opposed the war, including draft-age men who refused to go, soldiers and veterans who turned against the war and refused to fight, and students, trade unionists and other workers, African-Americans and other communities of color, women, the LGBT community, elected officials at all levels of government including Congressional representatives who eventually cut off funding for the war, even business people and many others .

The Vietnamese people's struggle ultimately won their freedom and independence, and ended the war. But the US anti-war movement played an important supportive role, helping win majority public opposition, encouraging and supporting war resisters, and pressuring Congress to cut funds. This photo exhibit shows some of the faces of this huge anti-war movement.

The anti-war movement comprised many thousands of acts by millions of Americans from all walks of life. Many leaders and activists in CCDS were leaders and activists in the anti-war movement 40 and 50+ years ago.

Nearly all these photos were taken by long-time anti-war and social justice activist, photographer, and CCDS member, Ted Reich.

We also recommend reading the CCDS book, "*Vietnam: From National Liberation to 21st Century Socialism*," to get the true story of Vietnam, including the history of the war, and the rebuilding of a socialist society today. Available at: lulu/changemaker.com.

The Editors

On April 17, 1965, Students for a Democratic Society called the first mass march on Washington to oppose the war in Vietnam. The turnout, some 25,000, far exceeded expectations, and set a long struggle in motion.

Well-known folk singers and other entertainers performed anti-war songs at many peace rallies and demonstrations across the country throughout the war years making a big contribution toward building the anti-war movement.

Here, left to right:

Phil Ochs, Judy Collins, Joan Baez, and Barbara Dane perform at the SDS march.

The SDS-led crowd filled the grounds of the Washington Monument, mostly with young people.

Protestors again march in Washington, D.C. May 15, 1966 to demand an end to the war and to include the National Liberation Front in a resolution to ending the war

Many prominent American leaders demanded an end to the war. Here, from left to right, is Andrew Young (civil rights organizer who later became a US congressman from Georgia and US Ambassador to the UN); Mrs. Spock; Dr. Benjamin Spock (famous pediatrician); and Martin Luther King, Jr. (civil rights leader.) They led a march to the United Nations in New York City on April 15, 1967 to urge world leaders to increase their opposition to the US war against Vietnam

Soldiers began to turn against the war. Demonstrators here demand freedom for the "Fort Hood 3" at the New York State Selective Service Headquarters, October 14, 1966. The three soldiers refused to fight in Vietnam, were convicted, and sentenced to prison. Their refusal to go to Vietnam sparked an upsurge in draft resistance and soldiers refusing to fight.

Labor opposition to the war also grew as the war intensified. Here, members and leaders of the United Electrical workers (UE) protest in Washington, DC. Union members were present from Cleveland, Ohio; Ft. Wayne, Indiana and many other cities and towns. One sign calls for a "Strike for Peace."

Vietnam Veterans Against the War march in New York City August 5, 1966.

Wives, sisters, girlfriends, mothers and supporters stage a sit-in at the Army Induction Center in New York City on May 26, 1967.

Protestors demand an end to the draft in front of the Armed Forces Recruiting Station in Times Square, New York City, September 13, 1967. The protest was organized by the W.E.B DuBois Clubs

Below: Police use tear gas against protesters as actions became larger and more militant.

The war created divisions at the top, and 'peace candidates,' such as Senator Eugene McCarthy, emerged to challenge the White House. Third parties also emerged, such as the Freedom & Peace Party, below, and the Peace & Freedom Party elsewhere.

Peace and social justice activists demand freedom for the Harrisburg 8 and Angela Davis in Harrisburg, capitol of Pennsylvania in April 1972. (Below) The Harrisburg 8 were religious leaders, led by Father Philip Berrigan, who opposed the war and who were framed on charges of conspiracy to kidnap Secretary of State Henry Kissinger. They were convicted and sentenced to prison. Angela Davis, a professor at the University of California and a member of the Communist Party, was falsely charged with conspiracy in connection with killings in a Marin County, California court in 1970. A world-wide protest campaign won her freedom. She later became a founding member of the Committees of Correspondence for Democracy and Socialism. The 1972 demonstration in Harrisburg was organized by the People's Coalition for Peace and Justice, the largest peace and social justice organization in the country

Why I Joined CCDS: An Appeal

By Paul Krehbiel

I joined the Committees of Correspondence for Democracy and Socialism because:

1. I wanted to be a part of an organization that was bigger than myself. I had been involved in many progressive, labor, anti-war, anti-racist and left campaigns but I felt a need to work together with other like-minded people to multiply my efforts.

2. I wanted to be a part of an organization that I agree with and feel at home within. There are many organizations on the left, and many do good work. But I felt at home in CCDS because it is an organization that is guided by principles and analysis that I agree with. CCDS is guided by Marxism but is not dogmatic, and is open to and supportive of the ideas of many other thinkers, and the actions of a wide array of social justice activists.

3. I wanted to be a part of an organization that is thoughtful, and encourages deep probing and questioning, and lively but friendly debate and discussion.

4. I wanted to be a part of an organization where members are rooted in mass movements and constituencies, and are really rooted among and with the American people and their organizations.

5. I wanted to be a part of an organization that gives special attention to the most exploited and oppressed, African Americans and other people of color, women and others who suffer discrimination. I want to be a part of an organization that is multi-racial, and reflects the diversity of the people of our country, knowing that it is right and makes us stronger.

6. I wanted to be a part of an organization that gives special attention to the working class, especially the labor movement and all working people.

7. I wanted to be a part of an organization that believes in coalitions, knowing that the left and people's movements are stronger when we work together in alliances, and is actively working to bring these alliances into being.

8. I wanted to be a part of an organization that believes in democracy, and uses deeply democratic practices, inclusiveness and transparency in all areas of its work.

9. I wanted to be a part of an organization that knows how to link reform and revolution, that understands how to fight for immediate popular reforms today in a way that lays the groundwork for achieving something better, ultimately a socialist society.

10. I wanted to be a part of an organization that believes in international solidarity, especially with working people and the oppressed all over the world, and those who have freed themselves from the domination of oppressors, both foreign and domestic.

11. I wanted to be a part of an organization that has a general path forward and is creative. It's important to have a plan to achieve a better society, and also to recognize that it is a work in progress. CCDS encourages creativity, and testing different ideas and approaches as necessary steps to progress along the road to real freedom.

12. I wanted to be a part of an organization that is made up of a lot of nice people, people who have mutual respect for each other, help each other, and become good friends with each other. CCS respects the individual, and the collective. It's a lot easier and more enjoyable to work in that kind of organization.

That's CCDS. Join me and many others. Join CCDS today.

We Need You to Join Us....

We're inviting you to join the Committees of Correspondence for Democracy and Socialism. We need your help in building a progressive majority for peace, justice and equality—and then pushing on to a new society where these will be the rule, rather than the exception. Socialism is being more widely discussed today than any time since the 1960s, and you can't take part in it fully without a socialist organization.

Working with many others, CCDS aims to end existing wars and prevent new ones. We oppose the current austerity being imposed upon the working people, a burden made even heavier by militarism and the hidden costs of non-renewable energy systems. We need a global order based on peaceful relations among nations, mutual respect and human rights, and the creation of economies that can exist in harmony with nature.

You can make a difference. Lend a hand in organizing with others to fight for a progressive agenda in the streets, workplaces, communities of faith and schools. It's not crowded up front, so sign up today!

Fill out and mail today.
_____ Yes, I'd like to join the CCDS. Enclosed is my check for: $ _____.
I'd like a subscription to Dialogue & Initiative. Enclosed is my check for $12.50 (Non-Members, $15.00).
I know good causes need money. Here is my contribution of $_____.

Name _____
Address _____
City _____ State _____ Zip _____
Phone_____ Email _____

Make check payable to Committees of Correspondence, and mail to: CCDS Membership, 6422 Irwin Ct., Oakland, CA, 94609

Email: national@cc-ds.org Web: www.cc-ds.org

The Committees of Correspondence for Democracy and Socialism (CCDS) is a national organization dedicated to the struggle for justice, equality, democracy, peace and socialism. The annual membership is $36 for individuals; $18 for unemployed, seniors, youth, and others with low income; $48 for households

Take a Free Subscription to Our Weekly E-Newsletter...

Easy to sign on and to unsubscribe as well. Go to http://tinyurl.com.ccdslinks, pick a back issue, and click the button in the left column. Arrives every Friday AM

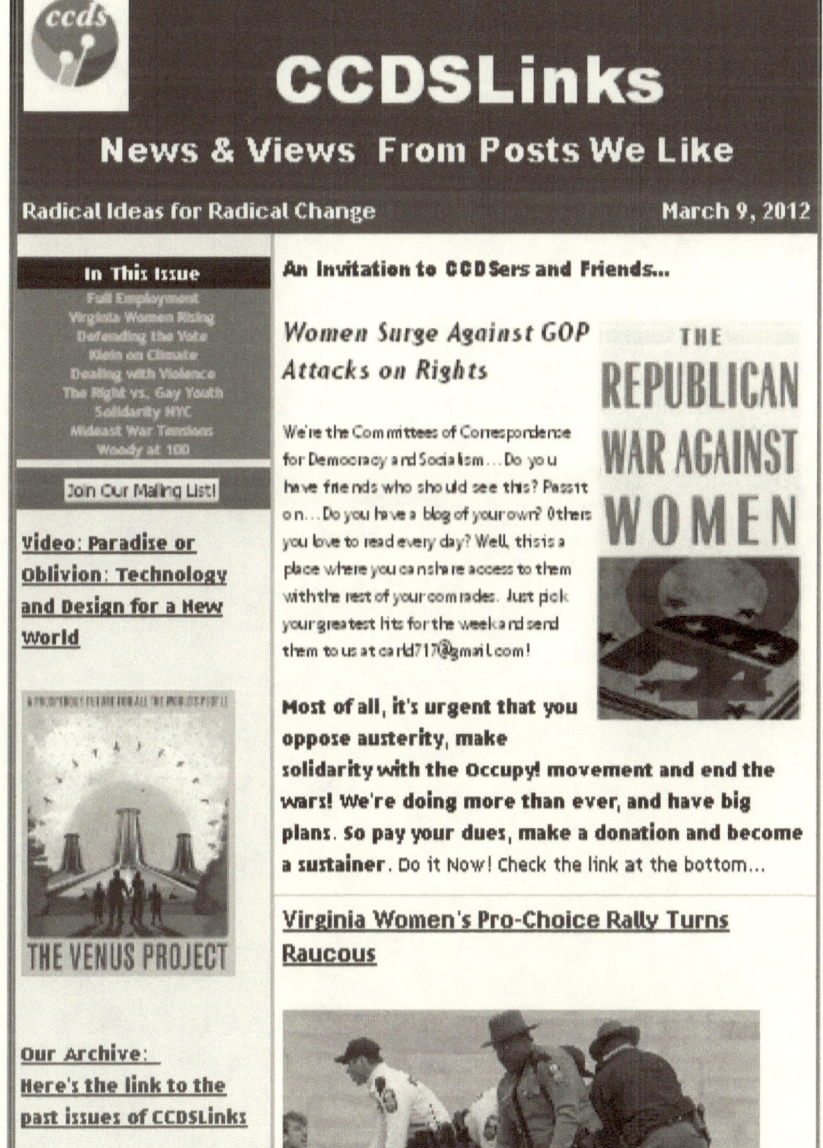

www.ingramcontent.com/pod-product-compliance
Lightning Source LLC
Chambersburg PA
CBHW032014170526
45157CB00002B/691